FRANK LLOYD WRIGHT'S HOUSE BEAUTIFUL

"AND AT THE BEGINNING OF STRUCTURE LIES ALWAYS AND

EVERYWHERE GEOMETRY. . . . THE CIRCLE [SYMBOLIZES] INFINITY;

THE TRIANGLE, STRUCTURAL UNITY; THE SPIRE, ASPIRATION;

THE SPIRAL, ORGANIC PROGRESS; THE SQUARE, INTEGRITY."

FRANK LLOYD WRIGHT, *THE JAPANESE PRINT: AN INTERPRETATION*, 1912

FRANK LLOYD WRIGHT'S

House Beautiful

DIANE MADDEX

HEARST BOOKS · NEW YORK

Library of Congress Cataloging-in-Publication Data
Maddex, Diane.
Frank Lloyd Wright's house beautiful / by Diane Maddex.
p.   cm.
Includes index.
ISBN 0-688-16736-5
1. Wright, Frank Lloyd, 1867–1959—Themes, motives. 2. Architect-designed houses. I. Title.
NA737.W7A4 2000
728'.092—dc21   99-36733
                                                          CIP

Printed in Hong Kong

10   9   8   7   6   5   4   3   2   1

Produced by Archetype Press, Inc.
Washington, D.C.
Diane Maddex, Project Director
Robert L. Wiser, Designer
Carol Kim, Editorial Assistant

The text of this book was typeset in Eagle, a typeface designed by Morris Fuller Benton in 1933 for the National Recovery Administration. A computerized version was prepared in 1994 by David Berlow and Jonathan Corum for the Font Bureau.

Endpapers: Adaptation of fabric No. 102, designed by Wright for F. Schumacher and Company and announced in the November 1955 *House Beautiful.* Drawing by Robert L. Wiser, Archetype Press

Page 2: Marin County Civic Center (1957), San Rafael, California

Page 3: Anderton Court Shops (1952), Beverly Hills, California

Page 4: Oak side chairs for the Boynton House (1908), Rochester, New York

Page 5: Wingspread (1939), Racine, Wisconsin

Page 6: Taliesin West (1937–59), Scottsdale, Arizona

Page 7: Ennis House (1923), Los Angeles, California

Page 8: Ablin House (1958), Bakersfield, California

Page 9: Hexagonal plywood tables for the Rayward House (1955), New Canaan, Connecticut

Pages 10–11: Pfeiffer House (1971) (based on Jester House project of 1938), Taliesin West, Scottsdale, Arizona

Page 13: A window for the Little House (1902), Peoria, Illinois

Pages 16–17: The ebony library of Glenview Mansion (1876, Charles W. Clinton), a Victorian house in Yonkers, New York

Pages 18–19: Wright's May House (1908), Grand Rapids, Michigan

CONTENTS

F O R E W O R D

LOUIS OLIVER GROPP

EDITOR IN CHIEF

HOUSE BEAUTIFUL

The very title of this book—*Frank Lloyd Wright's House Beautiful*—suggests the depth of the relationship between America's foremost architect and this country's oldest shelter magazine. Perhaps it was inevitable. Both the man and the magazine started out in the last decade of the nineteenth century, in Chicago, at a time when the country was ready for a new architecture for a new century. Both of them shared an ideal of the day: that a beautiful house would lead to a good life. *House Beautiful* began reporting on Wright's work in its third issue and never stopped. The magazine that described its editorial vision as a "missionary business" had found its prophet. ☐ The match made in heaven reached its apex in the 1940s and 1950s when a crusading editor in the tradition of the magazine's founders, Elizabeth Cordon, celebrated *House Beautiful's* fiftieth anniversary with a December 1946 story on "The Most Influential Design Source of the Last 50 Years," Frank Lloyd Wright. In the 1950s the architect joined forces with the editor in her battle against the International Style. The man and the magazine became a movement, offering up entire issues on Wright's work as the more American way of building. Controversial as they were, their efforts certainly helped establish Wright as America's preeminent architect. ☐ More recently, on the 125th anniversary of Wright's birth, with the restoration of his Guggenheim Museum, *House Beautiful* again remembered Wright, and for its own centennial issue in November 1996, the magazine recounted the role his work played in the century of design mirrored by the magazine. Now, with Diane Maddex's thorough and thoughtful book, their shared vision—that a beautiful house furthers the good life—continues into the twenty-first century.

Wright's fascination with geometry is clear in designs such as his Honeycomb House in Stanford, California, designed in 1936 for Paul and Jean Hanna. Like a beehive, the house is an ingenious fabric of hexagonal modules. The entry sets the mood "for a world of fluent patterns and interwoven light and shadow," noted *House Beautiful* in a special issue on the house in January 1963.

GONE...

homes designed as caves

rooms built as "boxes beside boxes or inside boxes"

empty grandeur intended to produce an inferiority complex

formal parlors saved for company

walls that block light and air

a separation between inside and outside

windows that look like holes in walls

a "festering mass of ancient styles"

pilasters, entablatures, and cornices

elaborate interior trim

useless mantels

open staircases that take up too much space

closets that become "unsanitary boxes wasteful of room"

fussy furniture

applied ornament

draperies "without rhyme or sanitary reason"

painted wood

wallpaper

visible light fixtures

gold-framed pictures with white mats

bric-a-brac

REPLACED WITH...

space designed from within

form and function joined as one

human scale

low walls that serve as screens

open plans

one large living area divisible as needed

an orientation to catch the sun

ties to nature through terraces, skylights, and outswinging windows

an integral fireplace

fewer doors

unified patterns and motifs

natural materials and colors

furnishings that are part of the whole composition

built-in seating and bookshelves

indirect lighting

dried flowers to bring nature inside

murals that integrate art into walls

"IF OUR INTERIORS COULD BE FITTED UP WITH

THE TRUEST SENSE OF THE FITNESS OF THINGS,

INSTEAD OF TRYING TO LOOK 'ARTISTIC' OR

INTRODUCTION: FRANK LLOYD WRIGHT

'ELEGANT' OR 'FASHIONABLE', WE SHOULD

FIND GREATER RECOMPENSE FOR OUR

LABORS AFTER BEAUTIFUL HOMES. LET ORNA-

MENT BE A NECESSITY, BUT LET IT BE THE

FLOWER OF HEALTHFUL NEED; LET EVERY USE-

FUL ARTICLE BE BEAUTIFUL FROM ITS FITNESS

AND EVERY ORNAMENT BE USEFUL BY ITS

NEED." *HOUSE BEAUTIFUL*, DECEMBER 1896

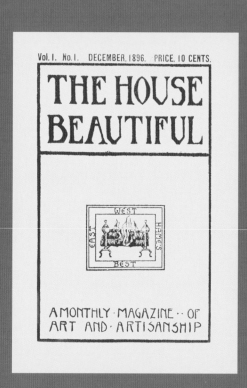

Frank Lloyd Wright and *House Beautiful* came of age together. Both the world-famous

architect and the century-old magazine launched themselves in Chicago in the last

decade of the nineteenth century. It was a time of revolution on the home front, and the

two enlisted in the campaign to rescue American houses from Victorian excess. Wright

rose through the ranks to lead the domestic-reform movement, assisted periodically

by the magazine over the next sixty years. Their mutually beneficial relationship was,

AND *HOUSE BEAUTIFUL* in addition to being exceptionally long,

perhaps the closest ever between an American architect and a popular magazine.

□ In 1893, the year in which Wright opened his independent architectural practice,

Chicago became the flash point for two opposing views of what modern buildings

should look like. Down on the city's Midway, a vast "White City" of temporary struc-

tures transformed the World's Columbian Exposition into a classical apparition

harkening back to the glory of Greece and the grandeur of ancient Rome. It was a

slap in the face to Wright's employer at the time, the noted architect Louis Sullivan,

who was poised to create a new architecture for the new century, not to retrace the

tired styles of an old world. This was a battle that Wright was soon to take on. His

comrades-in-arms included other reformers—politicians, ministers, labor leaders,

suffragists—all of whom thought that the architectural revolution should start at home.

A cult of domesticity had evolved during the Victorian era after the Civil War, one that viewed the home as a haven and the center of family life. Repulsed by the extravagances of Victorian houses, social reformers decided in the 1890s that simplicity at home would lead to moral and political rectitude. The surroundings in which one lived, they thought, would affect how one acted; and if one acted morally at home, then surely the wider world would benefit. A house beautiful would lead to a city beautiful, not to mention a beautiful spirit. □ The concept of "the house beautiful" had deep roots. John Bunyan used the term in *The Pilgrim's Progress*, published in 1678. Oscar Wilde and Mark Twain picked it up, as did the design writer Clarence Cook in an 1878 book of the same name. In 1895 Robert Louis Stevenson gave a new twist to the era's infatuation with the idea in his poem "The House Beautiful." One might live in a naked house on a naked moor, "bleak without and bare within," he suggested, but the earth itself is our true "hermitage," a home made beautiful by the unceasing dawn and dusk of new days and seasons. □ That same year a Unitarian minister, William Channing Gannett, published a pamphlet of his own thoughts on "The House Beautiful." Clergymen had long taken their stands on the moral values of the home, so his topic was not unexpected. Gannett, a friend of Wright's uncle Jenkin Lloyd Jones, also a Unitarian minister, caught the young architect's attention. In the winter of 1896–97 Wright and a client labored to turn Gannett's words into a handprinted work of art, framed in borders drawn in Wright's abstracted nature motifs. The resulting book, *The House Beautiful* (see pages 40–44), began Wright's lifelong habit of preaching his own ideas. □ Eugene Klapp and Henry Blodgett Harvey of Chicago had much the same idea. In December 1896 they brought out the first issue of a monthly whose masthead claimed that it was "the only magazine in America devoted to Simplicity, Economy, and Appropriateness in the home."

"BOTH THE ARCHITECT AND THE EDITORS OF THE FLEDGLING MAGAZINE SHARED A LATE-19TH-CENTURY IDEAL: THAT A BEAUTIFUL HOUSE FURTHERED THE GOOD LIFE, BOTH MORALLY AND AESTHETICALLY."
LOUIS OLIVER GROPP, *HOUSE BEAUTIFUL*, JUNE 1992

The House Beautiful magazine asserted in its inaugural edition that it saw "a radical necessity to have beautiful interiors—not gorgeous, not fashionable, but useful and harmonious," if for nothing else than the edification of children. Klapp, an engineer and architect, sold the magazine the next year to a Chicago publisher, Herbert S. Stone, who became its editor. □ Stone, like Edward Bok, publisher of the *Ladies' Home Journal,* and, soon, Gustav Stickley in his *Craftsman* magazine, looked to the home as a symbol of society and an incubator for reform. Drawing on the ideas of William Morris and his followers in the Arts

and Crafts movement, Stone hewed out a progressive editorial policy favoring not just restrained architecture but also popular democracy, public health, better urban housing, city planning, and women's rights. He presumed that most of his readers could not afford their own architects, so he pushed for standardization and mass production as a way to guarantee appropriate dwellings. Readers were advised to toss out their bric-a-brac and other fussy furnishings. □ By just the third issue, in February 1897, the magazine and the architect had found each other. Visiting "Successful Houses," *The House Beautiful* entered Wright's world in suburban Oak Park, Illinois, and became the first national magazine to feature one of his houses. Every room in the home he designed in 1889 and expanded in

Wright found time in the 1890s for a quiet moment on the tree-shaded veranda of his home in Oak Park, which *House Beautiful* visited in its third issue. "The arrangement of the windows," wrote the reporter in February 1897, "is purposely such as to cause the rooms to depend largely on the outside for part of their charm."

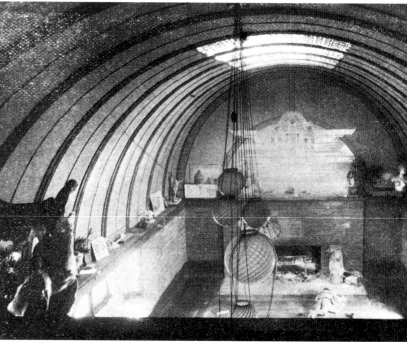

1895, said the writer, "has been arranged with the intention of obtaining a complete composition." A "most austere simplicity" prevailed in the dining room, "there being absolutely no unnecessary furniture." As radical as Wright's dining room was, the upstairs playroom for his children (ultimately six) was "the most remarkable of all." Little more than two years later, the magazine returned to the compelling household of Frank and Catherine Wright to inspect the architect's new studio and revisit the revolutionary dining room, its furnishings all designed by the owner to make the room a complete work of art. "It is refreshing," concluded Alfred H. Granger, "to come in contact with a genius so fresh, so truthful, and so full of vitality." Only three years after its founding, *The House Beautiful* had recognized the genius in its midst. Others in Chicago and beyond were about to. □ Wright, who was born in Richland Center, Wisconsin, on June 8, 1867, arrived in Chicago just before his twentieth

When *House Beautiful* first published Wright's Oak Park home in February 1897, it showed readers two views of the "remarkable" playroom he had added for his children (above). "The first impression on standing in the door," the magazine noted, "is of the great height of the ceiling, forming a perfect half-circle." In December 1899 it returned to tour the library in Wright's new studio (opposite left), which was added in 1898, and the family dining room (opposite right), with its tall-back spindled chairs.

birthday. The great fire of 1871 had opened up vast architectural opportunities, and this

refugee from engineering school was eager to build. He apprenticed first with Joseph

Lyman Silsbee, a family friend, and then in 1888 obtained a coveted position with Adler and

Sullivan, one of the key shapers of American modernism. But skyscrapers, the firm's

"IT WAS JUST AS IMPORTANT FOR HIM TO HAVE A

specialty, held less appeal for Wright at the time. America's true monument, the most

pressing problem to be solved, he believed, was the home. A family's residence was the

BEAUTIFULLY ARRANGED BREAKFAST TABLE AS IT

symbol of democracy and individualism to him, and Wright took it as the major challenge

of his entire seventy-two-year career. He completed more than three hundred houses

WAS TO BUILD A BEAUTIFUL BUILDING." ELIZABETH

and designed a hundred more that never left the drafting board. Because he focused so

clearly on where and how we live, he captured the imagination of people around the world

GORDON, *HOUSE BEAUTIFUL*, OCTOBER 1959

and today lives on as the household name for architect. ☐ Wright had to leave Louis

Sullivan's employ because he was found to be moonlighting on the side to make money—

and because above everything else he wanted to design houses, a rare commission in

Sullivan's office. On his own after 1893, Wright spent the century's last years articulating his vision in bricks and mortar as well as in words. He began to speak to women's clubs and

civic groups, carrying the social reformers' cudgel to "make the whole world homelike," as

the temperance advocate Frances Willard put it. The reformist views made a perfect plat-

form from which to launch his own developing principles. In 1897 he became a charter

member of Chicago's Arts and Crafts Society, aligning himself in many respects with the

followers of Morris who favored "artistic" homes with simple and useful things. Wright's war

"ARCHITECTURE IS PRIMARILY INTERIOR; *OF*

of words continued for all of his ninety-one years, and he was not shy about using whatever

means came his way. □ *The House Beautiful* caught up with him again in 1906, five years

THE THING, NOT *ON* IT. IT IS NOT A DEAD ASPECT

after the *Ladies' Home Journal* published two of Wright's innovative designs. Together with

a group of other progressive architects in Chicago and the Midwest, Wright had been

OF STYLE BUT *STYLE* ITSELF, BEARING EVER FRESH

toiling to express his own idea of the house beautiful. It should, he said, respect the broad

line of the midwestern prairie, hugging the earth under a wide, sheltering roof with an

FORM, LIKE ALL LIVING THINGS IN NATURE."

open plan and expansive windows that blur the distinction between indoors and out. And

it should grow organically from native soil just like a wildflower on the prairie. This new

FRANK LLOYD WRIGHT, *HOUSE BEAUTIFUL*, JULY 1953

school of architecture that Wright and his contemporaries built became known as the

Prairie style. The plan published in the February 1901 issue of the *Ladies' Home Journal* for

"A Home in a Prairie Town" synthesized his ground-breaking ideas. Another slightly more

traditional model house followed in July 1901. By 1906 *The House Beautiful* looked to

Wright in June, July, and August to solve a variety of house-building problems: how to

design for a seemingly unbuildable site (Wright loved the challenge); how to make the

In early residences such as the Charnley House of 1891 in Chicago,
designed while Wright was working for Louis Sullivan, the old
and new worlds of architecture melded gently. From Rome came
classical arches, and from Sullivan came the inspiration for the
sinuous woodwork in this urban villa. But Wright left his signature
in the ribbonlike bands of wood leading the eye from wall to wall.

most of a narrow lot (he was a genius at it); and how to design for middle-class home-

owners whose household help had joined the domestic revolution (his love of simplicity

made this a breeze). ☐ Wright's Hardy House in Racine, Wisconsin, wrote C. E. Percival in

the June 1906 issue, stood firmly on its bluff "like an object of art upon its pedestal." As he

told the magazine's 40,000 readers, "For one thing, the owner or the archi-

tect, instead of covering his entire lot with as ambitious a pile as he could

contrive, left ground enough to make a proper setting to his house." For

those who had to live a simpler life in "A House without a Servant," Percival

reminded them in the August 1906 issue that "with decorative windows, [a]

big fireplace, built-in seats and bookcases, a house is already half furnished."

Wright's buildings were beginning to speak for themselves. ☐ Throughout the

twentieth century's first decade, these same progressive ideals were echoed

in *The House Beautiful's* prose—in words such as *simplicity, beauty, useful-*

ness, harmony, restraint, freedom, progress, lastingness, artistic houses,

comfort, and *convenience.* "We are conducting a missionary business," the magazine

admitted in June 1912. By then the offices had been moved to New York City, and Stone left

his editorship the next year. But the "monthly magazine of art and artisanship" continued to

feature the work of the new Prairie School designers, even though it also addressed its

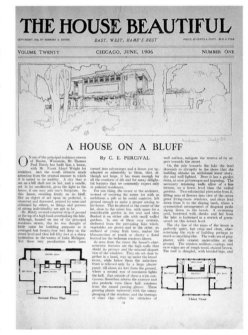

Wright's ground-hugging Robie House of 1908 in Chicago (opposite) was the culmination of his productive Prairie years. With
its cantilevered roofs, broad terraces, and overhanging eaves, it
symbolized shelter to many people. Bands of art glass windows
dancing with geometric patterns brought nature right into the
house. The Hardy House of 1905 in Racine, Wisconsin, featured in
"A House on a Bluff" in the June 1906 issue of *House Beautiful*
(above), proved Wright's skill at making the most of difficult sites.

readers' appetites for a variety of residential and decorating styles. Robert C. Spencer Jr.,

an architect who was a Wright friend, wrote some twenty articles in five years and was

succeeded by Charles E. White Jr., one of Wright's draftsmen and a popular commentator

on the Prairie movement. It was not the last time that Wright would have friends at the

magazine. ☐ After exhausting himself turning out Prairie-style masterpieces—including the

Willits, Dana, and Robie Houses among the more than one hundred commissions that

were built—Wright departed for Europe in the fall of 1909 with one of his former clients,

Mamah Borthwick Cheney. The ostensible purpose of Wright's voyage was to oversee

publication of his work by the German publisher Ernst Wasmuth, but the forty-two-year-old

architect was in actuality worn out, bored with family life, and in love with a new woman.

Triumph on the world architectural stage followed the Wasmuth portfolios, but at home his

flight marked an end to his most acclaimed period and the beginning of a dry spell when

Wright's name was no longer a household word. ☐ By World War I the Prairie style was out

and revivals were in—colonial, Tudor, Spanish, everything from the past that Wright's "new

school" wanted to banish. *House Beautiful* readers (the magazine lost its "The" in 1925)

preferred the familiarity of traditional houses. Neither the magazine nor Wright had much

good to say about the streamlined Art Deco or machinelike Bauhaus forms rising in

Europe. Issues in the 1930s showcased "American Modern," a less radical concept that built

on Wrightian principles of organic architecture. ☐ Wright's *magnum opus* during these

fallow years was his own second home, Taliesin, built in the rolling hills of Wisconsin where

he had spent much of his youth. Started in 1911, shortly after his return from abroad, the

spreading limestone house was conceived as a retreat from the world where he and

By the end of the Prairie period, his own country home in Spring
Green, Wisconsin, where he summered as a boy, became Wright's
new architectural laboratory. Taliesin, a Welsh word meaning "shin-
ing brow," always pulled him back, he said, "like some rubber band."

Mamah could live in harmony with the land. Tragedy put an end to that hope within three years, when a servant murdered her, her two children, and four others trapped inside Taliesin and set the house on fire. Both Wright and his home survived the conflagration, with scars, but thereafter he took commissions where he could get them—for Midway Gardens in Chicago, begun in 1913; for the grand Imperial Hotel in Tokyo from 1916 to 1923; and in the early 1920s for five exotic houses built around Los Angeles, four of them using Wright's novel system of "textile" blocks fashioned of concrete. □ In January 1941 *House Beautiful* gained a dynamic new editor, Elizabeth Gordon. Within a few years she wrote to Wright, who was then spending summers at Taliesin and winters at Taliesin West, his desert home in Scottsdale, Arizona, which he had begun in 1937. Yousuf Karsh was taking portrait photographs of "great architects" for the magazine, she explained in October 1944. "I didn't know," replied Wright, "there were great architects, so I shall stay on the sidelines an interested spectator. Thank you nevertheless for the inference." □ Gordon visited Taliesin West

in April 1946 in preparation for *House Beautiful's* fiftieth-anniversary issue, scheduled for December, as well as for a shorter feature, "Meet Frank Lloyd Wright," in June (illustrated—finally—with a Karsh portrait). Gordon had plans to honor Wright as the magazine's "ideological founder." As she wrote in August: "If a publishing rebellion went hand in hand with your architectural revolution, we would like to know it and record it." □ Once the December issue appeared, Wright told Gordon that he had been "crowned"; the issue was a "very fine tribute indeed." He

was only being modest, as usual. *House Beautiful* heralded him as "the most influential design source" of the last fifty years, noting that the "whole concept of designing a house from the inside, for the greatest possible good of the occupants, started with Wright." The architect opened the doors to his desert home—"a symphony composed of sun and shadow"—while the magazine concluded its twelve-page feature on it by stating that "the indispensable ingredient in architecture, as in life itself, is the creative act. The rest is

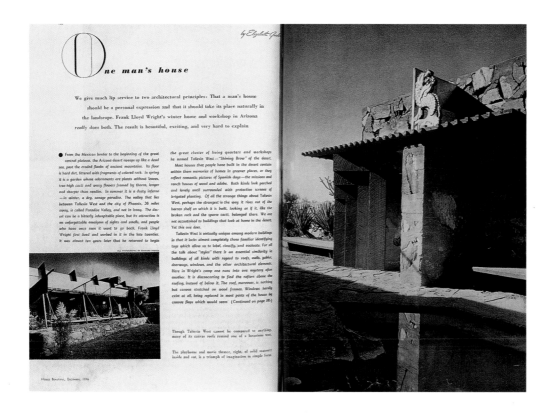

simply a kind of window-dressing." ☐ Wright was back, rediscovered by *House Beautiful*

and an eager public. He had paved his own return in the mid-1930s with one of the most

"[WRIGHT IS] THE GREATEST ARCHI-

important designs that he ever "shook out" of his sleeve. Fallingwater, the house built over,

not beside, a waterfall in Mill Run, Pennsylvania, landed him on the cover of *Time* magazine

TECT ALIVE—OH, WHY NOT SAY IT, THE

for January 17, 1938. *Architectural Forum* devoted its entire January 1938 issue to him, and

the same year *Life* featured one of his model homes. As a result of his *Autobiography*,

GREATEST ARCHITECT WHO EVER

published in 1932 and revised in 1943, a new generation of clients clamored to have him

design his moderate-cost houses for them. A new wife, Olgivanna, and his new Taliesin

LIVED." *HOUSE BEAUTIFUL*, JUNE 1946

Fellowship, designed to let beginning architects learn by doing, buoyed his spirits. A retro-

spective of the seventy-three-year-old architect's work at the Museum of Modern Art in

Within several years of her arrival in 1941 as *House Beautiful's* new editor, Elizabeth Gordon reignited the magazine's relationship with Wright. They met at Taliesin West (opposite) while she was researching 1946 features inviting readers to "Meet Frank Lloyd Wright" and to look around "One Man's House" (above). The camp's canvas roofs, said the magazine, conjured up a "luxurious tent."

1940–41 helped seal his reputation as the godfather of modern architecture. □ The written word spoke for Wright almost as powerfully as his own buildings. He was later to confide to Elizabeth Gordon a statement made to him by a French architect: "It is no longer necessary for an architect to know construction. He must know journalism. If he is a good journalist, he will succeed." Wright asked her (he often called her Beth; she called him Mr. Wright) if architecture had "sunk so low," but in fact he was as skilled with words as he was with his T-square and compass. *House Beautiful's* issue of April 1953 would put him—and the magazine—to the test. □ That springtime issue sent a chill through the world of design. In what the magazine's editors today call their "most controversial editorial ever published," Gordon suggested that "something is rotten in the state of design—and it is spoiling some of our best efforts in modern living." As she described it, "The Threat to the Next America" was an International Style movement that carried with it the prospect of "cultural dictatorship." *House Beautiful* readers, she said, did not want the modernists' stripped-down emptiness, lack of storage space (and lack of possessions), meager kitchens, clinical Bauhaus furniture, or walls of unshaded glass like those Mies van der Rohe had recently chosen for the Farnsworth House in Illinois. The proponents of the pared-down style, Gordon said, were "a hair-shirt school," "a cult of austerity," "frauds and phonies," "a self-chosen elite who would dictate not only taste but a whole way of life." Less was not more, she added; it was simply less. She sent an advance copy to Wright. □ A telegram soon arrived. "Surprised and delighted. Did not know you had it in you. From now on at your

"THE 'INTERNATIONAL STYLE' IS NOTHING BUT THE OLD ARCHITECTURE OF THE BOX WITH ITS FACE LIFTED. ANY BOX IS MORE A COFFIN FOR THE HUMAN SPIRIT THAN AN INSPIRATION."

FRANK LLOYD WRIGHT, *HOUSE BEAUTIFUL*, JULY 1953

Elizabeth Gordon's April 1953 editorial in *House Beautiful* was a call to arms for all those who feared that the International Style would turn houses into glass boxes on stilts or make life sterile inside. One of her most sympathetic readers was Wright: a telegram from the "Godfather" offered his services to the magazine.

service. Godfather." The Phoenix dateline made it clear who shared her views. Just a few days later, however, he pointedly asked her why she had described the play of *Hamlet*—but left out Hamlet. "Am more than willing," she replied, "to put Hamlet back into *Hamlet*." At eighty-six, he returned to the stage. ☐ In the July 1953 issue *House Beautiful* gave Wright a forum to state his own views on the International Style. He appeared again in October to try to quiet some of the public outrage over the allegation that subversive political views motivated those searching for a modern language of architecture. "Without *individuality*," he told his critics, "architecture too soon hardens into static, frozen forms and becomes a Style. When our way of life thus hardens into a frozen thing, there is the end of democracy." From the 1893 World's Columbian Exposition in Chicago to the current controversy, Wright had promoted an architecture of, by, and for Americans over imports of foreign styles. In "the war that has been brewing since 1929, openly declared by a woman editor's scream," for Wright it came down to freedom—the sanctity of the individual versus collectivism, spiritual qualities versus machines for living in, the freestanding single-family home versus

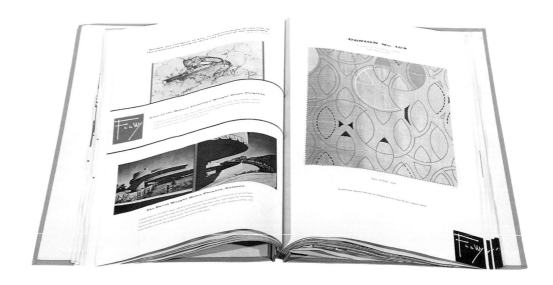

faceless apartment blocks. □ Before this watershed year was half over, Gordon had asked

Wright to suggest someone to replace one of her editors, James Marston Fitch. Responding

that it was "a great opportunity for *House Beautiful,"* Wright urged one of his apprentices,

"THE TRUTH IS THAT NATURE IS PRESENT IN THESE

John deKoven Hill, to join the staff. As its architecture editor and then executive editor for

the next decade, Hill began to explain Wright's way of building to *House Beautiful* readers,

BUILDINGS AS MUCH AS IT IS IN THE FLOW OF A

writing with the knowledge of an insider but the clarity of a true interpreter. He even

designed model rooms showcasing Wright's principles of organic architecture. "Mr. Wright

WATERFALL, THE GROWTH OF A PLANT AND THE

was happy I was there as a representative of the cause," he told *House Beautiful* in June

1992. Within a few years other Taliesin architects—Curtis Besinger, Kenneth Lockhart,

ROCK FORMATION OF A MOUNTAIN GLEN." JOHN

Byron (Robert) Mosher—added their voices to Elizabeth Gordon's crusading spirit. "We

were more than a magazine," Gordon later recalled. "The architecture department was an

DeKOVEN HILL, *HOUSE BEAUTIFUL*, NOVEMBER 1955

extension of Taliesin." □ In Wright *House Beautiful* found the "surest, steadiest and

strongest guide we now have for the road we all seek to a new poetic architecture." It was

At Elizabeth Gordon's urging, Wright in 1955 developed a line of
home furnishings for people who did not live in one of his houses.
Schumacher's Taliesin Line of fabrics and wallpapers (above)
was announced in the November 1955 special issue of *House
Beautiful* devoted to Wright. That same issue illustrated the modular furniture he designed for Heritage-Henredon (opposite).

a statement, the magazine admitted in January 1957, "verging on idolatry." The association between the two was an architect's dream. A model Usonian house erected in New York City in conjunction with the 1953 Wright retrospective *Sixty Years of Living Architecture* was furnished courtesy of *House Beautiful.* A 1954 exhibition at the Los Angeles County Fair, *The Arts of Daily Living,* was sponsored by the magazine to promote "a more beautiful life" and dedicated to Wright. In November 1955 a mammoth special issue of *House Beautiful* featured his work in detailed illustrated articles. That same year, at the instigation of Elizabeth Gordon, a line of home furnishings designed by Wright and his associates allowed average homeowners to bring a touch of Wright into their own houses. □ The November 1955 *House Beautiful* called Wright "the man who liberated architecture." Its hundreds of advertisement-rich pages looked at his principles, his innovations, the poetry of structure in his hands, the importance of the site and landscaping, the eloquence of his materials, how he used space ingeniously, how he made each home a work of art—even his love for

music, film, and parties. It toured an early Prairie masterpiece, the Coonley House of 1907 in Riverside, Illinois, and took readers inside Wright family homes—the rugged Taliesin and his sons' circular and elliptical fantasies—not to mention Fallingwater, Wright's answer to the International Style. Behind the scenes at every turn, Wright was clearly a master of journalism as well as of wood, brick, stone, and glass. □ He died in Phoenix on April 9, 1959, two months before he would have completed his ninety-second year. *House Beautiful* commemorated his passing in October with another robust issue that assessed "the creative genius as well as the fighting power of this remarkable man. For he was," it added, "as much a crusading social thinker as he was a designer." Wright's Usonian masterwork, the Hanna House in Stanford, California, took over the entire January 1963 issue. Many of its words came from Paul and Jean Hanna, two of the legions of grateful homeowners who kept Wright's memory alive. By October John deKoven Hill returned to Taliesin, and in December 1964 Elizabeth Gordon retired after more than two decades as *House Beau-tiful's* editor. Not just in her tenure but throughout its long history, Gordon had written in

The most "lived-in" room in our house

We both do a great deal of desk work, and this room coddles us with conveniences and feeds us with beauty.

It is the center of our workaday life

● We are so happy with our library that we cannot imagine today how we were able to get along with our original tiny study. Only the thought that it was temporary must have sustained us. We couldn't even have a fireplace in the original room, though we had the under-pinnings installed when we built the original house. Today there may actually be as many as twelve weeks of the year in which we fail to have a fire in our library fireplace.

The library today is the result of removing a temporary wall and combining the original study and original master-bedroom. The result was, as Mr. Wright said, "to open up the back of the house to match the openness of the front." It is possible to sit in the library and look straight through the TV room and master-bedroom to the back terrace. While the children were growing up, we believed the living-room playroom area to be the most beautiful and satisfying part of the house. It is still beautiful and satisfying, but has been superseded in our affections by the warmth and richness of the library-master-bedroom area.

The entire east side of the library is a glass wall with three sets of double doors opening directly onto the terrace. As we said before, there are no shades or curtains to obscure our view of the terrace, the hillside, and the cascade-pool. The two of us usually eat breakfast in the library—the morning sunny side—and dinner at night in front of the fire. We have literally moved to the back of the house. The size of the room permits two huge desks, cabinets for type-writer and adding machine, files, display cabinet, a couch, and comfortable chairs. The walls are lined with book-shelves; the ceiling holds overhead lights, roll maps, and a suspended globe. We spend countless happy hours on research and writing in this most satisfying and inspiring room. It is an invitation to work.

It becomes a small living room in which to entertain three or four guests; it is a room for conferring with students, a playroom for grandchildren. It *(Please turn the page)*

This view of the library tells more than the view on the front cover, because you see where the garden is. This is the center for daytime living because this is the east-facing side. So it is a sunny and cheerful place until the mid-afternoon.

Then the other side of the house (living and dining room) becomes the compelling side. Printed cotton upholstery on the couch under bookcases was a "find" in Jaipur. Our twin desks provide ample space for our research and writing projects.

House Beautiful, January 1963

1959, the magazine had "tried to edit by Wrightian precepts and principles." □ Back in May 1953, just when those precepts and principles were becoming fighting words for *House Beautiful,* Wright was honored by the National Institute of Arts and Letters. "You have built not one but many Emersonian mousetraps," read the citation, "and the world has enthusi-astically beaten a well-worn and widening path in merited appreciation." He was, said the institute, a Prometheus, a Moses, a true pioneer, but especially "a blithe spirit with more of Puck than of Ariel" who designed buildings "as if they were to take their place in a happier world—one of light, of grace, of gaiety. . . . " Wright had viewed himself that year as Hamlet, but his fellow artists may have had the keenest insight of all.

"HERE IS A NEW ARCHITECTURE FOR A NEW WORLD."

JOSEPH A. BARRY, *HOUSE BEAUTIFUL,* NOVEMBER 1955

House Beautiful's coverage of Wright did not end with his death in April 1959. The editors assessed his legacy in a special issue in Oc-tober (opposite left) and then followed up in January 1963 with de-tailed coverage of "one of the truly great houses in America," Wright's Hanna House of 1936 in Stanford, California (opposite right and above). Paul and Jean Hanna related that building this house had been "one of the greatest adventures" of their lives.

THE HOUSE BEAUTIFUL:

"A ROOM AS IT IS USUALLY KEPT IS [AN] INDEX OF ONE'S TASTE, OF ONE'S CULTURE, AND

OF A GOOD DEAL OF ONE'S CHARACTER." WILLIAM C. GANNETT, *THE HOUSE BEAUTIFUL*, 1896

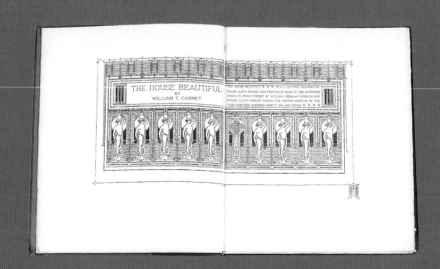

Beauty is "as mysterious as life," admitted Frank Lloyd Wright in 1910. Attempts to define it are foolish, he added, noting, "We instinctively feel the good, true, and beautiful to be essentially one in the last analysis." Beginning in 1894, when he was twenty-seven, Wright spent a long lifetime trying to define the indefinable: what makes a house beautiful. He liked to talk and write about the subject almost as much as he liked to design. His speeches and writings today spill out of more than five thick

PRINCIPLES TO BUILD ON

volumes. The first book with which he was associated, however, featured not his own words but those of another preacher, the Reverend William Channing Gannett. □ It was called *The House Beautiful*—after Gannett's sermon and the popular domestic ideal of the day—and it was printed by Wright and his client William H. Winslow during 1896–97 and into 1898 (with the minister's name misspelled on the title page). Just three years before, as his first private commission, Wright had designed Winslow a daring new house in River Forest, Illinois; they used Winslow's press in his Wrightian stable to produce their limited-edition book, one that no doubt would have appealed to the great Arts and Crafts printer William Morris (who died the year their project began). Wright wove carpetlike borders to frame Gannett's words with intricate abstractions drawn from nature and added nature photographs of his own. The link of sermon to book was apt in more ways than the obvious. Like Morris and his followers, Wright wanted to make all things beautiful. And a book, to him, was what a cathedral was to the middle ages. "It embalms for us in type the qualifications of our time," he said in 1896.

Gannett's sermon in Wright's cathedral proclaimed, however sentimentally, principles

dear to the hearts of the architect and fellow reform-minded idealists. A beautiful house

"THE IDEALS OF BEAUTY ARE FOUND IN SIMPLE, REST-

was an outward symbol of inner peace and family harmony, "a world of strife shut out; a

world of love shut in," as Gannett exhorted. "The ideal of beauty," he suggested, "is simplicity

FUL THINGS FAR OFTENER THAN IN ORNATE THINGS."

and repose—not flash, not sensation, not show, not exaggeration, not bustle." But even

more than "walls and roof, chairs and tables and spoons," Gannett saw something else that

WILLIAM C. GANNETT, *THE HOUSE BEAUTIFUL*, 1896

was needed to turn a house into a home. He called it "the dear togetherness": warm light

from kind eyes, gentle tones, and thoughtfulness for one another—all comforting rays like "morning sunlight outside falling on quiet dewy fields." □ Simplicity and repose were "blessed qualities" also to Wright, who singled out the phrase himself in his first documented speech a year before Gannett's sermon was initially published as a pamphlet in 1895. In the interests of household beauty, Wright urged, for example, that part of the meal

Wright and William Winslow printed their book *The House Beautiful* in the stable behind this golden brick house in River Forest, Illinois, that the young architect designed in 1893 for Winslow, his first private client. Some Sullivanesque details remain—in the dark terra-cotta frieze that makes the second story almost disappear and in the ornament ringing the front door and its side windows—but the bold, assured form of the house is all Wright's.

budget be invested in a flower for the table, all the better to feed the family spiritually in the long run. The savings from "dinners cheapened for a month," the reverend similarly advised his own congregation, "will make the bare dining-room so beautiful that plain dinners ever afterwards taste better in it." Two like minds met in *The House Beautiful.* □ Not as radical as he sometimes alleged, Wright's principles were rooted in fairly conventional late-nineteenth-century ideas of family, home, and community. Cities were teeming with immigrants from near and far, drawn to the riches to be had in the new industrial age. Laborers were marching for fair wages, feminists for equal rights, settlement workers for decent housing, politicians and doctors for better public health, mothers for temperance in drink. By 1893, when Wright became an architect on his own, home was where the world's problems would be healed. Suburbia's unspoiled nature beckoned as a green Eden. Politely nodding to its neighbors, the freestanding house was the nexus of family life, self-improvement, education, virtue, and culture. For Wright and other reformers, the house—more than the cathedrals of old—held out the hope of spiritual redemption. □ It had to be a simple one, however: easier to care for with women more frequently in the workforce and hired help harder to obtain; furnished with built-ins to conserve space; without plush upholstery to harbor germs and carved woodwork to gather dust. Simpler inside and out, the preferred house became more standardized—less a self-expression as in the Victorian era—and built for economy. New plumbing, heating, and electrical systems invaded the home. Even so it grew smaller, with fewer rooms but more open spaces and windows. The kitchen, thanks to

"SCRATCH OUT THE 'VERYS' FROM YOUR TALK, FROM YOUR WRITING, FROM YOUR HOUSE-FURNISHING."

WILLIAM C. GANNETT, *THE HOUSE BEAUTIFUL*, 1896

In Wright's hands, the housing-reform notions current in 1900 were shaped to unforeseen beauty. Critics agreed with him that his Willits House of 1902 in Highland Park, north of Chicago, was his first great Prairie house. Under the art glass ceiling light's soft glow, the dining room exudes the feeling of a woodland forest.

scientific housekeeping ideas espoused by writers such as Catherine Beecher at mid-

century, took over as the heart of the home. The machine became the family's friend.

Rooms were beautified with wildflowers or Japanese screens rather than eclectic objects.

The house beautiful would close the door on Victorian clutter and the looming chaos of the

modern world. "Inartistic homes," said one reformer, "ruin our manners and morals and

wreck our nervous systems." □ Into this domestic revolution strode Frank Lloyd Wright. The

"THE ARCHITECT'S BUILDING IS A MIRROR OF

reform manifestos melded nicely with the personal values that came with him from

Wisconsin, notably his respect for nature and his Unitarian family's belief in the unity of all

THE MAN, BUT ALSO A MIRROR OF THE VALUES

things. Just as important, Wright viewed architecture as civilization's greatest art, one

higher even than the music he loved. Because he saw it at the core of American democ-

OF THE SOCIETY HE LIVES IN." FRANK LLOYD

racy, Wright vested architecture with the power to accomplish social goals. He also shared

the Arts and Crafts movement's desire to make useful objects beautiful, although he

WRIGHT, *HOUSE BEAUTIFUL*, OCTOBER 1953

favored the straight-edged efficiencies of modern machines over more intricate handi-

craft. Yet the residences he designed—Wright said they were called "dress reform houses,"

as if fit for the new woman to wear—carry a signature that distinguishes them from the

houses of other architects. He transformed the ideas and ideals of his day into a new

language of architecture. It was not a style but a set of principles. The words—the materials,

the shapes—may have changed over seven decades, but the underlying grammar remained

constant. □ At both ends of his career, Wright produced houses that were designed from

Six decades into his career, Wright was still using his first principles—just dressed in new clothing. In 1944 Herbert and Katherine
Jacobs asked Wright to design his second home for them in Middleton, Wisconsin. He used natural stone inside and out, built in
bookcases and other furnishings to conserve space, and simplified
family life by combining activities in one open room. He burrowed
the walls into an earth berm on the house's public side but opened
the private side with a broad ellipse of windows to let the sun in.

within, beginning with the plan; that tore down walls to open up interiors; that were low and

sheltering, almost married to the ground; that were sited in harmony with nature; that

honestly expressed their materials and method of construction; that celebrated freedom

and reflected—even helped spur—new ways of living. Using his broad principles, Wright

created his own exceptional concept of what makes a house a home. For him, the house

beautiful: ☐ **BUILDS WITH NATURE.** "Go to Nature," commanded Wright in 1894 in

one of his first pronouncements. "Let your home appear to grow easily from its site." It

should be built *of* the hill, not *on* it, and look, he later explained, as if no one can tell where

the ground leaves off and the building begins. Nature is the soul of every Wright design, the

origin of its form and its ornament. For him, as for his heroes Emerson, Thoreau, and

"THE CHARACTER OF THE SITE IS THE
Whitman, it represented fertility and the freedom of American democracy itself. ☐ From

nature came Wright's idea that architecture should be organic, growing from within and

BEGINNING OF ARCHITECTURE."
opening like a flower to the sky. Flowers, plants, trees—these are the images that Wright

continually conjured up for his buildings. But he spurned naturalism, the realistic repre-

HOUSE BEAUTIFUL, **NOVEMBER 1955**
sentation of nature, in favor of abstractions that delved deep into nature's cells, into the

geometry of structure. Early on, Wright used the midwestern prairie as another metaphor for

nature. Its flatness compelled him to respect the landscape with shelter just as broad, low,

and open, thus indelibly tying the hand of the architect to the land. Form did not merely follow

function, as Louis Sullivan had suggested; form and function, countered Wright, are one.

"The Wrightian law is the law of nature," said *House Beautiful* in
November 1955. Water particularly inspired him: at the 1949
Walker House in Carmel, California (top left), at the 1955 Rayward
House in New Canaan, Connecticut (bottom left), and at Taliesin,
his 1911 Wisconsin home (bottom right). Most buildings hugged the
ground. A berm at the Jacobses' 1944 house in Middleton, Wisconsin (top right), pulls up close as protection from chill winds.

□ **TAKES ITS DESIGN FROM WITHIN.** Conceptualizing a house from the

outside—based on a historical style, for example—was not Wright's way. Forms from the

past, he said, were nothing but "tombs of a life that has been lived." Around the time he was

designing Unity Temple in Oak Park, Illinois, in 1905, it came to him that the reality of a

building was not its walls and roof but the space enclosed within them. The rooms thus

dictated the outward appearance. Inside and outside were no longer separate; they were

organically unified. This revelation, which Wright discovered had been suggested thou-

sands of years earlier by the Chinese philosopher Lao Tzu, shaped all of his buildings.

□ In his hands interiors turned into continuous spaces whose plasticity begged to be

molded rather than broken up with posts and columns, ornament and fixtures. Houses spoke to him not as caves but as "broad shelter in the open, related to vista; vista without and vista within." As one moves around, spaces seem to gain a fluidity of their own. Wright made buildings understandable best from within, and he made the interior space visible outside. As a result, the design focus changed from what passersby would think of the exterior to how the residents would experience their own house inside. ☐ **HAS A GRAMMAR OF ITS OWN.** Wright decided at the start of his career that every design element should grow from one basic idea, a motif adhered to consistently so that "each building aesthetically is cut from one piece of goods." From unity would come integrity,

one of his central principles. In later years he called this sense of order a house's own grammar, the system it uses to speak to the world. ☐ Wright usually deduced this grammar in nature, perhaps in a plant whose stylized stems and leaves would appear in art glass windows and reappear in lamps, cabinets, and table runners. Or he mirrored the plan of the house itself—a rectangle, a triangle, a hexagon—in furniture and inscribed it on floors and ceilings. Only with such consistency, he said, could a house truly be considered a work of art created by an artist. ☐ **USES NATURAL COLORS AND MATERIALS.** "Go to the woods and fields for color schemes," Wright instructed in 1908. The soft, warm, "optimistic" tones found in the earth and the forest greens, golds, and reds of autumn leaves suited him more than the ribbon counter's "pessimistic" blues, purples, and cold greens and grays. Wright liked the rich, natural hues of wood inside and out, from white and red oak to golden cypress and deep mahogany. Brick in tawny gold or muddy tan reflected the earth from which it came. ☐ Wright let his materials speak as honestly and naturally as his colors. He learned to see brick as brick, wood as wood, glass as glass, and not to force any one of them to be something it was not meant to be. The innate nature of materials should be respected, he admonished. Carving wood, for example, violated its nature, as did painting and varnishing it; staining brought out its inherent beauty. Nor did plaster's natural character need to be dressed in wallpaper. If buildings were above all as sincere and true as people, he thought, truth would produce harmony; in falsity's wake came only discord.

"EVERY MATERIAL HAS ITS OWN ELOQUENT MESSAGE, ITS OWN LYRICAL SONG, AND NO ONE HAS MADE THEM SING SO BEAUTIFULLY AS FRANK LLOYD WRIGHT."

ROBERT MOSHER, *HOUSE BEAUTIFUL*, NOVEMBER 1955

At Fallingwater, Wright's 1935 masterwork in Mill Run, Pennsylvania, rough-cut sandstone was laid in projecting layers to mimic its natural state. For contrast in color and texture, Wright molded luxurious terraces for the house and a zigzag stairway out of concrete, a material he loved for its inherently plastic quality.

□ **CELEBRATES GEOMETRIC FORMS DRAWN FROM NATURE.** Beginning in *The House Beautiful* book in 1896, Wright often characterized himself as a weaver who fabricated buildings on a unit system just as a rug's pile is stitched into the warp. The units he used were geometric, first squares and cubes, and then more complex forms such as hexagons and ellipses and sometimes circles. As a boy he had learned to see such patterns in nature by working with the wooden blocks developed by Friedrich Froebel. Ever after, nature for Wright was a tapestry of interdependent, related units, and geometry became the underlying grammar of his architectural language. □ **CONVEYS AN ORIENTAL SENSE OF SIMPLICITY.** Unlike some of his fellow reformers, Wright saw simplicity not as an end in itself but as a means to an end. Fewer rooms, fewer possessions, everything pared down, would lead to a simpler life. He sought the innate grace of a wildflower rather than the plainness of bones (as he called the International Style) or a barn door (Mission and Stickley furniture). The Japanese had it about right, he conceded, saying that he and they went to the same source: nature. □ The Japanese print, for one, "conventionalized" or abstracted life with a form of simplification akin to Wright's geometric abstractions of nature. And, like Wright's, Japanese houses were built with as few rooms as possible; movable screens eliminated the need for walls and opened the interior to nature. Needless objects were banished. The Japanese did not "outrage" wood but used it as nature supposedly intended. If building organically is more oriental than Western, suggested Wright, in this sense his work could be considered oriental.

From the plans of his houses down to the last decorative detail, geometry was Wright's mentor. At Aline Barnsdall's Hollyhock House of 1917–21 in Hollywood, bouquets of abstract hollyhock stalks found their way into stone and glass. Triangles cascade asymmetrically on the house's windows, while stacked squares blossom along pillars and friezes inside and outside the house.

□ **INCLUDES FURNISHINGS AS PART OF THE WHOLE.** "It is quite impossible to consider the building one thing and its furnishings another," said Wright in 1910. Chairs and tables, windows and lights, even decorative objects were "mere structural details" of a house, variations on its theme. Like democracy's citizens, each contributed to the harmonious union. □ This ideal was one he shared with other architects, but Wright was more persuasive than most in achieving it. Wherever he could, he built in cabinets, bookcases, fireplace inglenooks, sofas, and tables and blended in "naked" radiators and other appurtenances of modern life. The rest of the furnishings were "at large" but coordinated in form, material, and color with the overriding motif of the house. When clients insisted on bringing their own furniture—"the horrors of the old order," he called them—it was often a painful affront to the architect. □ **INTEGRATES ORNAMENT INTO ITS MATERIALS.** For Wright, the weaver, ornamentation had to be "wrought in the warp and woof of the structure." It was never applied, like paint or wallpaper. He preferred to think in terms of patterns rather than ornament, natural patterns that grew organically from a house's materials, construction, or motif. Just as he viewed a symphony as an "edifice of sound," Wright extracted inner rhythms of form to energize his compositions. Bands of wood marched along walls and ceilings to create "eye music." Patterns molded into concrete built endless variations into "textile" blocks. Nature's geometry was frozen into art glass windows that cast ever-changing shadows inside. All that was needed to complete a home's decoration were some wildflowers ("because, to be a normally growing

When Wright's clients allowed him to design not just the house but everything in it as well, he could give each family a complete work of art. The May House of 1908 in Grand Rapids, Michigan, is one of his Prairie houses where nothing was left to chance. Even simple furnishings such as a rocker are extensions of the architecture.

thing is to be beautiful") and perhaps a classical statue or an oriental object to serve as

messengers from distant civilizations. □ **CREATES A SENSE OF REPOSE.** Begin-

ning in 1894 and continuing for the next half century, Wright complained that people really

did not know how to live in their houses. If home was to be the retreat from disorder desired

by the nineteenth-century reformers, homeowners had a duty, he said, to "raise the char-

acter and tone" of their houses to achieve a life of repose inside. Repose at home may

have been a male ideal, but Wright at least considered the effect of warring floors, walls, and

ceilings and quarreling forms and colors on the children of the house. They breathe a

house's atmosphere "as surely as the plain air," he noted, urging parents to build their resi-

dences with the same principles of truth, beauty, and consistency they teach their offspring.

Like the Reverend William Gannett, whose words he helped commit
to type in *The House Beautiful,* Wright thought that a home re-
quired more than mere walls. It had to invite repose and family
togetherness. Under live oaks laced with Spanish moss in
Yemassee, South Carolina, Wright in 1939 created a romantic
retreat named Auldbrass that mirrors the serenity of its location.

□ **PRODUCES HARMONY THROUGH UNITY.** "One thing instead of many things," Wright liked to say, "a great thing instead of a collection of smaller ones." If a house's materials and colors grow naturally from native soil, if it adheres to one grand theme and minor variations, if its furnishings and ornament are integral elements, then and only then will it have the unity of a well-composed symphony or an exquisitely painted masterpiece. His credo never changed: "I believe a house is more a home by being a work of Art." □ These were the building blocks of Wright's architecture, his way of making a house beautiful. He remained faithful to their spirit for nearly sixty-five years, as architectural fads came and went and a new century's styles percolated around him. As with any set of prescriptions, one can find some contradictions: Wright railed against styles, yet his own work naturally came to have the mark of a personal style. He sometimes built right *on* the land, not quite *of* it, as he instructed, and did not actually visit all of his sites before designing buildings for them. His

"PEOPLE WHO HAVE NEVER SEEN OR NEVER LIVED IN A BEAUTIFUL ENVIRONMENT, OR NEVER LIVED SURROUNDED BY THE QUIET HARMONY OF ORGANIC ARCHITECTURE CAN NEVER KNOW WHAT THEY HAVE MISSED." FRANK LLOYD WRIGHT, *HOUSE BEAUTIFUL***, OCTOBER 1954**

"moderate-cost" houses usually ended up costing too much. He spoke of each home-owner's freedom of expression but used his own vision to control "petty individualism," down to the table linens in some cases. He claimed that form and function are one, yet form was known to win out from time to time over watertight roofs and warm rooms. He lent his name to a commercial line of furnishings despite previously asserting that items should be designed for each house alone. He extolled repose yet devised furniture that bruised even his own shins. He recognized a young person's need to grow up in rewarding surroundings yet walked out on his first six children. □ Such dichotomies could be viewed as nothing more

"BECAUSE IT IS A WORK OF PRINCIPLE, IT IS HONEST,

than the contrasts he built into his own work: horizontal and vertical, dark and light, tension and release, glass and stone, wood and plaster, open and closed, inside and outside, the

AND BEING HONEST, IT IS BOTH ELOQUENT AND

work of humans and the work of nature. Wright was a romantic visionary who divulged in 1896 that he wanted to create houses that were "biographies and poems . . . appealing to the

QUIET." LOREN POPE, *HOUSE BEAUTIFUL*, AUGUST 1948

center of the human soul through perceptive faculties as potent as those that made the book." He always wove a good tale, around his houses as well as himself, while reaching for integrity—his own "Truth against the world," as his family motto commanded. □ A few years into the twentieth century, Avery and Queene Coonley asked Wright to be the architect of their home in Riverside, Illinois, because, he wrote in his 1932 *Autobiography*, they saw in his houses "the countenances of principle." Spurred by the compliment, he put his best into their house. For hundreds of clients who followed the Coonleys, the same steadfastness shone through as Wright put his principles to work.

Perforated wood screens like the pair used on a bedroom window of the Pope-Leighey House of 1939 in Mount Vernon, Virginia, allowed Wright to build pattern naturally into his houses. "An American home," he prophesied in 1896, "will be a product of our time, spiritually and physically. It will be a great work of art, respected the world over, because of its integrity, its real worth."

"A MOST RADICAL DEPARTURE":

"I HAVE CALLED MR. WRIGHT A RADICAL OPPONENT OF THE USE OF ANCIENT STYLES.

WHILE HE CARRIES HIS OPPOSITION TO ANTIQUITY TO A FAR GREATER EXTENT THAN

MANY OF US CAN AGREE WITH, IT IS REFRESHING TO COME IN CONTACT WITH A GENIUS

SO FRESH, SO TRUTHFUL, AND SO FULL OF VITALITY. . . ." ALFRED H. GRANGER,

HOUSE BEAUTIFUL, DECEMBER 1899

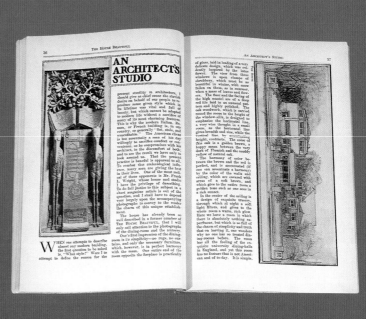

As Wright began to design houses, first in Louis Sullivan's office in the early 1890s, then completely on his own after 1893, he struggled to form a picture in his mind of what a modern house should be. He knew clearly what it should not be, and he said so in 1894 and 1896. For a start, homeowners should avoid "something which will rear on its hind legs and paw the air in order that you may seem more important than your neighbor." □ Instead, the modern house should grow from its site, with

WRIGHT'S FIRST HOUSES

no basement, no porch, and no "excrescences" on the roof. It was to be simple, harboring only as many rooms and possessions as necessary. The living room, designed around a fireplace, was the heart of the house; a "sunny alcove" might serve for the dining room. Furniture and lights were built in, and decoration was limited to "one really fine thing" and nature's bounty. Wright said no to a parlor saved for company (a "vaudeville stage"), to "vicious" furniture, to bric-a-brac, to "unsanitary" draperies, and to pictures "hung in effigy upon the walls." Spindled screens took the place of some solid walls. Simplicity and repose were his chief ideals. □ His own 1889 home in suburban Oak Park became the laboratory for his evolving ideas. Two years later, for Sullivan's firm, he produced a sculptural urban villa for James and Helen Charnley in downtown Chicago. On his own in 1893 he gave William Winslow a striking mansion in River Forest whose facade seems as formal as a classical column. Although the young architect was still taking on remodelings and an eclectic group of commissions to pay the bills, Wright's growing mastery of bold masonry forms came to the fore with the Heller House of 1896 in Chicago. His motto at the time was that "there should be as many types of homes as there are types of people."

FORM AND FUNCTION

When Wright looked around him in the 1890s, he saw not houses but "bedeviled" boxes with

fussy lids and holes punched out. It became his mission to tear down their cell-like walls

and let their residents live free. For his metaphor he chose screens—movable, ornamental,

and translucent to light, just as the Japanese used them. Windows metamorphosed into

light screens, eliminating the boundary between indoors and outdoors, and walls served

principally to enclose the space within. □ These ideas entered his vocabulary gradually in

"MANY ARCHITECTS MAKE THE MISTAKE OF BEGIN-
his first decade as an architect. The basement, with its "blinking" eyes peeking out, was

discarded in favor of a solid platform on which a house could rise directly from the earth.

NING AT THE WRONG END AND TRYING TO MAKE
Wall coverings slid over the frame like flesh on bones. Surfaces were sculpturally divided

into zones. Windows came together to function as one lookout on the world. And above,

FLOOR PLANS TO FIT SOME PRECONCEIVED SCHEME
seeming to float in freedom, a broad roof gave meaning to the word *shelter*. □ Inside,

human scale prevailed. Ceilings were low where people sat—at the fireplace, over the

OF EXTERIOR." *HOUSE BEAUTIFUL*, JUNE 1905
dinner table—and, to stress their importance, higher where they stood. Vistas expanded, as

space flowed around half-walls and spindled screens. Wright tried to make walls, ceilings,

and floors continuous surfaces, one melding into the other through similar textures, colors,

and wood trim. As doors and partitions disappeared, the downstairs became essentially

one living room, focused around a hearth located at the house's core. Some old forms

remained—an arch here, a gable there—but the new order was beginning to emerge.

Wright's shingled home in Oak Park, Illinois, designed in 1889, was the place in which he tested many of his architectural ideas. It was the first house of his to be built, and although it borrowed some late-Victorian features, it broke new ground architecturally. The snaking walk, the hidden entrance, and the oversize gable on the front all set the house apart as the work of an independent mind. "The whole place has the effect of a well-balanced picture," said *House Beautiful* in February 1897, the magazine's third issue.

Up the steps, between the rotund urns, beneath the crouching stone figures, past the

playful stork sculptures, then a choice of doors—Wright made an adventure out of visiting

the studio attached to his Oak Park home in 1898. Guests always knew when they finally

found the entrance to one of his buildings that they had truly arrived. Advance, recede, turn

once, then again. He made everyone dance as the password to enter. □ This was a secret

game that Wright discovered a little way into his career, but his deep interest in the act of

entering a building is apparent even early on. The typical house of the era, he claimed, had

"an especially ugly hole to go in and come out of." Once he found that he could mold a

facade, that it did not have to be merely a "wall-building," he was able to view a door as

more than a separation between outside and inside. In the flat-faced Winslow House of 1893

(see pages 42–43), Wright pinpointed the front door with an ornamental white mask over-

laying the taut brick skin, its pair of windows outlined like eyes around the waiting mouth of

a door. Inside a house, he liked to offer "a warm shake of the hand to those who entered

there." □ The Japanese were expert at Wright's kind of intricate march to the entrance. Visi-

tors might leave the public sphere via a bridge to enter the private life of a house,

announced by a cloistered courtyard. The route could be mysterious and winding, but in fol-

lowing the path of discovery one saw the light of the architect's plan and became part of it.

By 1898, when he added a studio to his home, Wright had become adept at gently shepherding visitors to the door (top left).
Inside the house (top right), wood spindles screened the stairs in
the hall. Visitors to the Heller House of 1896 in Chicago (bottom
left) were met, up several short flights of steps, by a monumen-
tal Sullivanesque entrance. Its hall (bottom right) offered a choice
of dining room to the left, stairs up, or living room to the right.

Wright thought of lakes as nature's mirrors and used glass to catch similar reflections from

sky and trees to incorporate into his buildings. By the early 1900s he became renowned for

geometric art glass windows that trapped nature right in the panes, but in his first houses

Wright was still trying to decide what to do with windows. In the Winslow House of 1893 they

are obviously little more than its "eyes." Soon Wright was to find that windows could

become the building itself. □ Plate glass became more readily available in the United

States by the mid-1880s, about the time Wright was beginning his career. This new tech-

nological advance was "the gift of gifts," he recalled in 1930, a material that signified the

freedom of "ancestors living in trees." With glass he was able to build light right into a wall

and eventually to make walls and ceilings virtually disappear. It was his most important tool

in breaking down the boxes people had been living in. Combining windows in bands, wrap-

ping them around corners, and opening them to nature with outswinging casements

emphasized the plasticity of his architecture and increased the sense of space inside.

□ Sullivanesque nature patterns appear in his first forays into decorative windows—in the

dining alcove of the Winslow House, for example, and the stair hall of the remodeled

Roberts House of 1896 in Oak Park. His own dining room pulled an abstracted lotus pattern

out of a plan book. But upstairs in his children's playroom, fields of squared tulips on either

side of the dramatic space hint at the great art glass to come. And in the Heller House of

1896 the grouped and sculpted bands of windows are more than stuck-on "eyes": they

begin to express the house's own internal organization.

Art glass windows filter light and geometric patterns into the playroom Wright added in 1895 for his children. "It cannot be ques-
tioned," said the February 1897 *House Beautiful,* "but that children
brought up in a room like this, with its simple beauty and strength
as a daily fact, will little by little feel its influence and come to
regard it as only natural that all rooms should be as this one is."

TRUTH IS LIFE.

GOOD FRIEND, AROVND THESE
HEARTH-STONES SPEAK NO EVIL
WORD OF ANY CREATVRE

In the days before central heating and electricity, a family gathered around its hearth for warmth and light. Many homes were little more than a fireplace boxed in, one writer claimed, making the family gathering spot a domestic altar. By Wright's time household technology was diminishing a fireplace's *raison d'etre,* yet the symbolism of togetherness and protection continued to be powerful, so the fires remained lit. □ A hearth was the heart of the house for Wright, who was comforted "to see the fire burning deep in the solid masonry of the house itself." He wanted real fires in a fireplace built into the core of a house—not a sham mantel stuck on a wall around a few coals in a grate. His fireplaces vented into a single chimney that was broad, generous, and low to the roof, a visual anchor for the house. □ The Arts and Crafts movement of Wright's era adopted the medieval custom of building a fire in an inglenook, a toasty inner sanctum whose benches framed the hearth. As both a place of retreat and a center of hospitality, the inglenook served Wright's needs for private and public domestic spaces. In his Oak Park home a small curtained nook in the living room, complete with a traditional homily, pays homage to family and friends. An arcaded inglenook at the Winslow House, raised three steps above the entrance hall, is an elaborate stage set as exotic as a harem. This regal hearth is the true center of the house, the pivot point for its pinwheel plan. Wright's theatricality was indelibly forged in the fire.

"THE FIREPLACE IS IN AN ALCOVE AT THE RIGHT OF THE ENTRANCE, AND IS MOST UNUSUALLY GRATEFUL IN ITS EFFECT. . . . THE ALCOVE IS JUST DEEP ENOUGH TO ALLOW OF A SHORT BENCH AT EACH END OF THE MANTEL, WHICH ADDS TO THE VERY COMFORTABLE APPEARANCE." *HOUSE BEAUTIFUL,* FEBRUARY 1897

A cavelike arch, crowned by a fan of red brick, contained the fire in Wright's Oak Park home. Upholstered benches encouraged the family to linger a bit. More arches appear at the Winslow House of 1893 in the neighboring town of River Forest (pages 72–73), but here they are not on the fireplace. Instead, they form a delicate arcade that screens the inglenook as if it were a separate room.

BUILT-IN FURNITURE

Pursuing his dream of making each home a work of art, Wright sought to build in as much furniture as he could. With furnishings firmly attached to his walls, there would be "complete harmony, nothing to arrange, nothing to disturb: room and furniture an 'entity.'" Sofas, tables, bookcases all became minor actors in his dramatic tableaus. It was not a new idea—Arts and Crafts devotees and housing reformers of the day also espoused them—but Wright took built-ins to a level of refinement seldom seen before or since. □ In his very first

"ONE SOMETIMES FINDS UNFORTUNATES TO

house, the one he designed in 1889 for his new wife, Catherine, and himself, he had willing clients. As *House Beautiful* observed when it visited in 1897 and again in 1899, the Wrights

WHOM . . . THE SHOW OF THEIR FURNITURE IS

enjoyed padded benches by the fireside and padded seats beneath the living room windows. Built-in shelves provided a home for their books while they added rhythm to the

OF MORE IMPORTANCE THAN ITS USE. . . ."

walls, a play of light against dark. In the children's playroom, added in 1895, toys could be stored beneath low window sills. And in the family's new dining room, Wright's most accom-

WILLIAM C. GANNETT, *THE HOUSE BEAUTIFUL*, 1896

plished space to date, he tucked cabinets and radiators along the wall and hid the electric light in the ceiling, to shine out through a fret-sawn screen as sunlight sifts through leaves in a tree. The room, reported *House Beautiful* in February 1897, was "a most radical departure from tradition." □ As for the rest, the less superfluous furniture the better, said Wright, not coincidentally to stave off inappropriate relics that his clients might treasure and pieces that forced wood into unnatural acts. Everything else not built in had to play the composer's tune of unity as well.

Beneath windows framed by wood columns and Sullivanesque swirls in the glass, the Winslows enjoyed built-in seating in the breakfast nook of their 1893 home in River Forest, Illinois (top). At the Wrights' Oak Park household (bottom), "the ampleness of the window seats," *House Beautiful* reported in February 1897, "does away with the necessity for a great many chairs, which only clutter up a room, bringing in conflicting elements of many styles."

Stuffed to the rafters, too many houses of his day seemed to Wright to be "mere notion stores, bazaars, or junk shops," as he complained in 1894. Early photographs of his own Oak Park home show that even the architect of simplicity originally had problems divesting himself of valued possessions. Decoration is dangerous unless one understands it, he conceded, later noting that it "is intended to make use more charming and comfort more appropriate." For him, learning to build pattern into a structure was the true poetry of conception. ☐ Interior walls of his houses became rich, mellow surfaces of natural tones, blooming with texture. These solid-color "paintings" were firmly built in, eliminating the need for the owners' pictures. Backgrounds for the life inside the house, Wright's natural canvases were framed by wood bands climbing vertically to stretch a room's height and flowing horizontally, usually at the door-top level, to visually tie one space to another. ☐ Wood screens were one of Wright's earliest ornamental devices. Their positive and negative patterns—there and not there—made walls drop out at intervals around a stairway or above a bookcase and added light and shadow to the decorative palette. Soon Wright was to transfer this tool to chairs with tall backs designed to screen the act of dining. An oriental rug or a carpet of quiet color and dignified weave, natural textiles such as linen or flax, a small classical sculpture, a Chinese vase, a Japanese print, a bouquet of wildflowers or leggy weeds (to Wright's hero Emerson, weeds were just plants "whose virtues have not been discovered")—and the house was furnished. Every item was organically integrated, a "voluntary sacrifice to an ideal."

"TO HIM, ORNAMENT ON A BUILDING WAS AS NATURAL AS PLUMAGE TO A BIRD, BLOSSOMS TO A PLANT, OR MUSIC AND POETRY TO THE HUMAN SPIRIT." *HOUSE BEAUTIFUL*, OCTOBER 1959

Intricate wood patterns showing Louis Sullivan's influence can be found in Wright's early houses, such as the Charnley House of 1891 in Chicago (top left) and the remodeled Roberts House of 1896 in Oak Park (top right). Even the dining room (bottom left) and playroom (bottom right) of his own home bear a debt to Sullivan in their recessed lighting fixtures. The Charnley House's stairway screen (pages 78–79) testifies to Wright's mastery of light and dark.

"STRETCHED UPON THE COUNTRY GRASS":

"ROOMS SHOULD BE IN THEMSELVES RESTFUL,

QUIET PICTURES, BACKGROUNDS FOR THE

LIFE WITHIN THEIR WALLS. THE SENTIMENT OF

IT ALL IS COMFORTABLE REPOSE, ELEGANCE

WITHOUT LUXURY, PRACTICAL COMPLETENESS

WITHOUT UGLY LINES. AND *NO JUNK!*" FRANK

LLOYD WRIGHT, *HOUSE BEAUTIFUL*, JUNE 1906

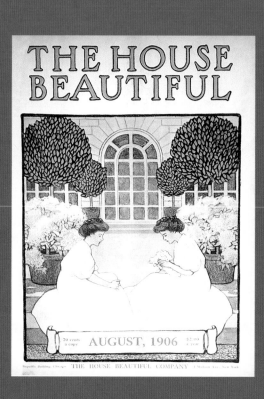

By 1900 the midwestern prairie—symbol of the supposedly endless American frontier—had almost vanished in the rush to claim land for homesteads. But in the prairie Wright found a potent metaphor for the new houses he envisioned. Its extended horizontal plane, he recollected toward the end of his career, was "the true earth-line of human life, indicative of freedom." These grassy lands represented the earth-bound simplicity he craved; their trees, flowers, and sky were "thrilling by contrast."

AT HOME ON THE PRAIRIE

☐ Wright, about two dozen other midwestern architects, and eager clients helped popularize the Prairie style nationwide until World War I. The sage of Oak Park, however, was the movement's undisputed leader and consequently was rediscovered by *House Beautiful.* From 1900 to 1910, and occasionally after that, his Prairie houses grew to love the earth: parallel to the land, accentuating its "quiet level," with sheltering eaves under gently sloping roofs, simple skylines, low terraces, and private gardens hidden behind outreaching walls. As C. E. Percival rhapsodized about Wright's Glasner House in the August 1906 *House Beautiful:* "So might a man stretch himself lovingly upon the country grass who would stand erect and alert upon town pavement." ☐ All vestiges of "the box" vanished, as rooms inside dictated what the outside looked like. Using cruciform and pinwheel plans, Wright projected space—containing it no more within four walls. He experimented with new technology from electricity to reinforced concrete. He succeeded in giving interiors the open vistas of the prairie. He began to design furniture as rectilinear as his walls. And he discovered a way as never before to capture nature in memorable art glass windows. With everything he did, Wright set the prairie on fire.

In Wright's first published plan for a Prairie house, it is the roofs that call out for a closer look. "A Home in a Prairie Town," offered to readers of the *Ladies' Home Journal* in February 1901 as a model modern house, rests securely under multiple roofs sheltering the bedrooms, the living area, the side terrace, and the porte cochere. Raised against the prairie sky, they could be treetops shading the trunk of the house. □ Just like branches, Wright's roofs were cantilevered past the walls to almost touch the landscape. "The horizontal line is the line of domesticity," he said in 1910, and nowhere is this as apparent as in his Prairie roofs. Usually hipped, but sometimes gabled or flat, they express the need for protection while they extend themselves in a gesture of nature's freedom. With the attic gone, roofs were released to stretch out low, in league with the ground like Japanese houses. □ The roof soffits (undersides) were typically painted a light color to reflect light back into the rooms. The sun's rays were further coaxed inside by expansive banks of windows beneath the roof, some even turning corners. As if by magic, glass dematerialized a wall and allowed the roof to appear to hover effortlessly above. The boxiness of post-and-beam construction was gone, replaced by support embedded within the building and only a pretense of it shown outside by assertive piers and low walls that stop well short of the brilliantly cantilevered roof. From their roofs on down to their foundations, Wright's houses—reminiscent of the architect himself, who liked to dress in a broad-brimmed hat floating above a flowing cape—were as well clothed as he always was.

"THINK OF THE ROOF AS AN UMBRELLA AGAINST THE SUN, WHICH CAN BE PIERCED AT REASONABLE JUNCTURES TO LET SHAFTS OF LIGHT AND SUN MARCH ACROSS THE FLUID INTERIOR SPACE BELOW." ELIZABETH GORDON, *HOUSE BEAUTIFUL*, OCTOBER 1959

Built down the street from his own home, the Thomas House of 1901 (top) was Wright's first Prairie house in Oak Park. For the Davidson House of 1908 in Buffalo, New York, he used hipped roofs again but made them almost as flat as the prairie. In both designs the broad overhangs seem to be set free by the miracle of glass.

As an architect who built with nature, Wright wanted each of his buildings to be "a grace, not

a disgrace, to its environment," he told *Esquire* in 1958. He intermingled house and site so

that each was the better for it. Private terraces carved out of urban neighborhoods,

gardens with architectural pergolas, glassed-in conservatories, flower boxes, French doors,

generous windows, plant and flower motifs, natural colors, and cut branches for decoration

all put residents in nature's bosom. □ At many Prairie houses, terraces became a lasting

symbol of Wright's reach out to nature, their low walls projecting from the house to enclose

"IT IS DIFFICULT TO SAY WHERE THE GARDEN

the outdoor space as part of the architecture. In Laura Gale's 1909 home in Oak Park—as

at Fallingwater three decades later–balconies powerfully thrust the building into the land-

ENDS AND THE HOUSE BEGINS IN ANY GOOD

scape. Wright also sought to recall informal prairie landscapes in his clients' gardens with

native trees such as oaks and elms, hardy flowers such as hollyhocks and daylilies, rocks,

ORGANIC STRUCTURE—AND THAT IS ALL AS IT

and built elements that mirrored the land's flat horizon. On terrace walls nature's bounty

overflows circle-in-square planter urns. □ Nowhere did house and hill merge as at Taliesin,

SHOULD BE." *HOUSE BEAUTIFUL*, NOVEMBER 1955

Wright's 1911 country home. Cultivated flowers and trees seem to grow from the rustic lime-

stone walls, themselves almost part of the land. Walls, garden courts, seats, fountains,

pavings, and planters ascend Wright's own hill in a romantic sequence that turns nature into

a protective outdoor room. At other sites such as the Glasner House, built on a ravine in

Glencoe, Illinois, and the Hardy House on Lake Michigan in Racine, Wisconsin, both visited

by *House Beautiful* in 1906 when they were new, Wright took advantage of nature as he found

it. But where clients did not have such breathtaking surroundings, Wright elevated their main

living areas to take in the best view they could get.

Landscaped courtyards such as Taliesin's in Spring Green, Wisconsin, allowed Wright to turn a family's attention inward. Water
added needed serenity to his urban gardens, notably in corners
of the Dana-Thomas House of 1902 in Springfield, Illinois (page
86), and the Allen House of 1916 in Wichita, Kansas (page 87).

NATURAL MATERIALS AND COLORS

Although some Prairie architects such as Walter Burley Griffin were challenged by rough-cut stone, Wright tended to limit his kit of exterior materials in this period to brick, stucco, and board and batten because of the seamless, almost plastic, surface they afforded. He was not beyond a "fireproof" reinforced-concrete house, however, proposing one in 1907 (again in the *Ladies' Home Journal)* as a domestic counterpart to Unity Temple in Oak Park, then in progress. Wright reserved stone—blocks of limestone laid as they came from the quarry—for Taliesin, his own experimental home in Wisconsin, begun in 1911 at the tail

"THE BAKED CLAY OF BRICK, THE GOLDEN

end of his Prairie triumphs. □ Whatever material Wright used, he used it naturally, without

forcing it to speak a different language. To fuse a material with a building's form and

GRAIN OF WOOD, THE SOFT TEXTURE OF STONE

method of construction was to arrive at the state of simplicity he desired. Bricks, often the

narrow Roman type, communicated rectilinearity; with their vertical joints mortared flush

ARE LIKE COLORS FOR HIS PALETTE." ROBERT

and colored to match the brick, and their horizontal joints raked to bring out shadows,

Wright emphasized the horizon of the prairie. On his taut stucco houses, wood bands

MOSHER, *HOUSE BEAUTIFUL,* NOVEMBER 1955

traced the underlying framing while they echoed the prairie's flat plane, as did horizontal

boards fastened by narrow battens on still other houses. □ Light and dark contrasts

continued inside, where wood strips outlined naturally colored plaster walls (no wallpaper,

thank you) that brought nature's autumn golds, rusty reds, and leafy greens indoors. At

Taliesin, the stone walls of the exterior became the interior backdrops as well, blurring the

distinction between nature and the protected space within.

Wright liked stucco for the way it covered walls as if it were plastic. At the 1902 Willits House in Highland Park, Illinois, he punctuated key features with contrasting dark bands of wood. In the dining room (pages 90–91), soft green walls, golden glass in the ceiling, and mellow oak tones take diners on a walk in the forest.

Inside his Prairie houses Wright finally got rid of "the box," as he called any house that

preceded him. Before Wright, people moved through halls to enter and leave a room by

one door. After him, they could almost float through their houses, moving in a circle through

living areas whose walls had pretty much vanished. Freed from their boxes, family members

were drawn together architecturally. ☐ Wright typically turned old-fashioned cubes of

houses into symmetrical cruciform or asymmetrical pinwheel plans, each of which looks

like its name and projects interior space in arms beyond the confines of four square walls.

The first floor, with its entrance, living and dining rooms, and kitchen, became essentially

one large living area, the heart of the house (the second level, if it afforded better views,

sometimes served this function). At the pivot point was the fireplace. Off to the side the

stairs rose to the second floor, which Wright begged not be dressed in "shabby under-

clothing" but be as well clothed as the first. ☐ He saw his rooms as protective retreats as

well as open tents where "every vista terminates with an agreeable prospect," as the July

1906 *House Beautiful* observed. From the primordial hearth to ceilings that soared, attic-

free, to the rafters, Wright built in multifaceted tensions and contrasts, changing levels and

pushing down ceilings in some areas to maintain the feeling of compression and release he

liked. Where wall and ceiling met, he might literally bring the sky and trees inside with a high

clerestory window. To emphasize the screenlike nature of these spaces, Wright divided the

walls with vertical wood strips to create "folded color planes." More wood bands affixed hori-

zontally topped the doors and windows and paralleled the floor, to bring walls and ceilings

down to human scale and tie one room to another with what he called "plastic-ribbons."

"IT IS A WRIGHTIAN PRINCIPLE THAT IF YOU CON-
FUSE THE BOUNDARIES OF A SPACE AND MAKE
THE PLANES IRREGULAR SO THE EYE IS NOT SURE
WHERE THEY ARE, YOU HAVE MADE THE SPACE
BIGGER OPTICALLY, TO SAY NOTHING OF MORE
INTERESTING." *HOUSE BEAUTIFUL*, OCTOBER 1959

Freed to be his own client at Taliesin, Wright decided to make the
dining area just a "sunny alcove" of the larger living room. Along
the sides of the room, windows frame expansive views of hills
and valleys, while a tented ceiling pushes the room toward the sky.

9 3

SHIMMERING ART GLASS

More than brick, plaster, or wood, glass became Wright's most important material during

his Prairie years. It allowed him to furnish his buildings with light, pattern, and color all at

once. With his art glass windows, doors, clerestories, skylights, and matching lamps—crys-

tallizations of nature—Wright the weaver turned his Prairie houses into "shimmering

fabrics—woven of rich glass." □ Almost as much as the glass itself Wright loved the new

electroglazing process that allowed him to easily sketch a metallic screen on his windows.

Within this metal tracery he set iridescent and clear glass to form abstract renditions of

flowers and trees, the plan of the house, or the geometry of nature he saw all around him.

For privacy—and to remove any need for a stuffy "mass of millinery"—patterns were more

complex at the bottom. The flat motifs played up the thinness and two-dimensionality of the

glass and made Wright's windows stay "severely 'put,'" not mixed up with the views outside.

□ Casement windows, with their uninterrupted frames for glass and their ability to swing out

to nature, made the perfect canvas for Wright's geometric wizardry, opening and closing

like folding screens of glass. Grouped together beneath the roof, art glass windows became

an architectural frieze of built-in ornament decked out in modern-day clothes. Skylights

and ceiling lights hiding electrical fixtures often played variations on the glass theme inside,

filtering light softly into the rooms and making ceilings disappear just as windows helped

the walls vanish. And through these lights incorporated into the building's fabric, shadows

choreographed a daily dance that kept Wright's houses alive with perpetual rhythm.

In motifs from squares to circles and in colors from sunshine to sunset, Wright produced screens of light at the Darwin Martin House of 1904 in Buffalo, New York, as well as in the Coonley Playhouse of 1912 in Riverside, Illinois (page 96), the Robie House of 1908 in Chicago (page 97, top left), the Dana-Thomas House of 1902 in Springfield, Illinois (top right), and the Little House of 1912 in Wayzata, Minnesota (bottom left). His famous Tree of Life window (bottom right) was also designed for the Martin House.

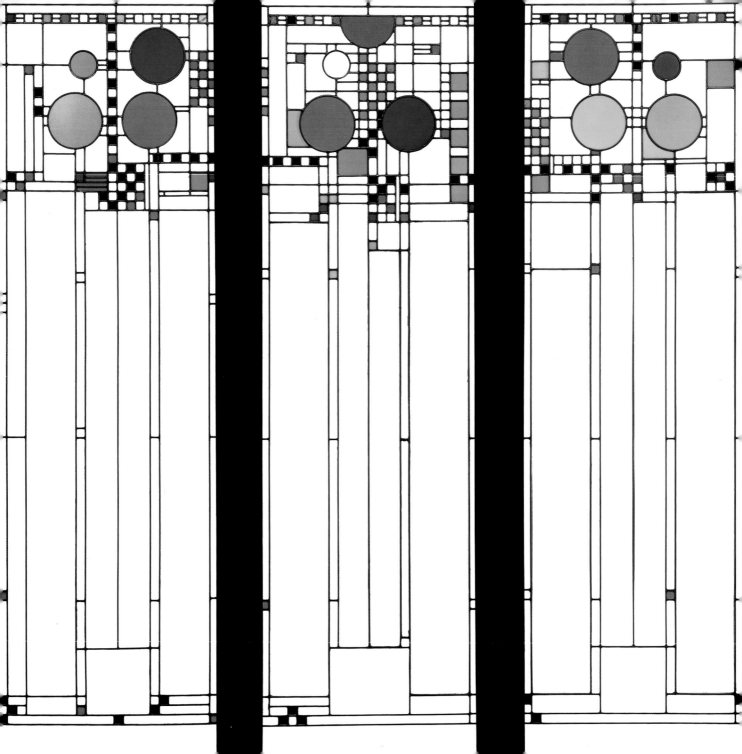

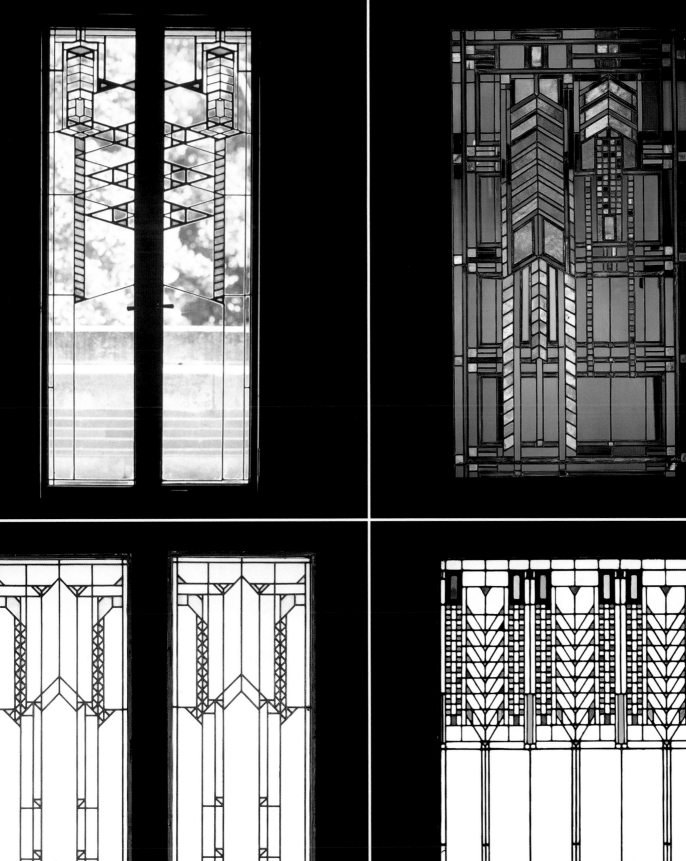

PROMINENT FIREPLACES

Wright usually moved the family hearth out from its cozy inglenook in the Prairie years and

made it "the heart of the whole and of the building itself." While his art glass windows

directed sunshine inside, the fireplace radiated sunny light and warmth back into the main

rooms (including some bedrooms). Its opening was broad and cavelike to reflect the prim-

"THIS GENEROUS FIREPLACE OF ROMAN BRICK, THE

itive attraction of fire—a fine psychological contrast to Wright's wide-open plans. ☐ His

fireplaces stood firmly on interior walls, where floor plans revolved around them. At the

SOLID BRICK HEARTH, THE BALCONY OVERHANGING

Robie House of 1908 in Chicago, Wright turned one face of the fireplace to the living room,

the other to the dining room to do double duty. The hearth itself was recessed below floor

IT, AND THE CHIMNEY ABOVE, PIERCING THE SLOP-

level, to weave it further into the building fabric. ☐ A number of Prairie fireplaces were

moon-shaped, as if to reinforce the cave symbolism, while most others hewed strictly to

ING CEILING, TOGETHER MAKE A COMFORTABLE

rectilinear lines, their skin relieved only by a slash of masonry lintel in lieu of a tacked-on

mantel. They were typically built of long, narrow Roman brick to recall the endless land-

FOIL FOR THE LARGE GLASS AREA OPPOSITE."

scape; Wright's twenty-three fireplaces at Taliesin were cut from the same rough limestone

as the walls. In the May House, Wright's 1908 Prairie gem in Grand Rapids, Michigan, he

C. E. PERCIVAL, *HOUSE BEAUTIFUL*, JUNE 1906

faced the horizontal rows of mortar with iridescent glass, turning the fireplace wall into gold

when the sun struck it (see pages 18–19). Fireplace hardware, from andirons to grates,

was just as carefully burnished with each house's design motif.

Wright sprinkled several hearths throughout Susan Lawrence
Dana's extravagant 1902 house in Springfield, Illinois. At one end
of her gallery, a barrel-vaulted space designed for entertain-
ing, he tucked an inglenook beneath a sparkling ceiling light to
bring the two-story room down to human scale. Like the brick
wall, two massive benches angle out as if making way for the fire.

Chairs, tables, lamps, tables with lamps, sofas, plant stands, music stands, Japanese print stands, night stands, beds—Wright designed them all in the Prairie years. He could not trust his clients, even those who knew a good architect when they saw one, to properly furnish his houses, and he abhorred "inferior desecrators." So the task of creating a total work of art fell to Wright himself. Oak Park studio employees such as Marion Mahony and the independent "interior architect" George Mann Niedecken of Milwaukee helped by serving as the "fingers" on the master's drawing hands. ☐ To fill in around the built-ins carried over from his first houses, Wright's office produced his signature spindled chairs with tall backs in numerous variations, solid-board slant-back chairs, and upholstered armchairs with slatted sides, more than a few of which Wright admitted made him "black and blue in some spot" from too-intimate contact. These hard right angles turned to curves in the famous barrel chair created for the Darwin Martin House of 1904 in Buffalo, New York. Wright invented new furniture when he had to—for instance, an ingenious table for viewing his beloved Japanese prints that he installed in Oak Park and later at the Dana and first Little Houses, designed sometime after 1902–3. ☐ Most of these pieces emerged in oak, which had previously been considered common. But in Wright's care, cut sparingly by machines and stained, not painted, to highlight the grain, they took their place as intrinsic building blocks of each house. In form and materials they were little sentinels of the architecture itself.

"SIMPLICITY IS ATTAINED BY AN AVOIDANCE OF CURVES, CARVINGS AND MEANINGLESS ORNAMENTS, AND BY LIMITING THE PIECES OF FURNITURE TO THE ACTUAL NEEDS OF THE OCCUPANTS, INSTEAD OF CROWDING THE ROOM WITH THEM."

C. E. PERCIVAL, *HOUSE BEAUTIFUL*, JUNE 1906

George Mann Niedecken assisted Wright with the furnishings of the Robie House in Chicago. Its most exceptional piece of furniture is the upholstered red oak sofa placed in the living room. Cantilevered outward on either side, the arms serve as built-in side tables. The slant-back chair on the left was a design Wright used frequently, but the tabouret table–footstool and its matching chair across the room were created especially for the house.

COHESIVE DINING ROOMS

Wright complained that sitting was an "unfortunate necessity," yet he overcame humans'

inelegance at it in the dining room. Beginning at home, with his own remodeled dining

room of 1895, and on into the first decade of the twentieth century, Wright turned dining into

"a great artistic opportunity." His Prairie-style dining rooms are some of the most cohesive

spaces he ever designed. □ Wright's achievement was due in large part to the chair—that

"THE PECULIAR FEATURE OF LIVING AND DINING

most difficult of furnishings—which at its core he viewed as a machine to sit in. So the

architect turned to the machine itself to manufacture modern thrones not with forced

ROOM IN ONE IS NO LONGER A FREAK OR AN

hand carving but with simple rectilinear lines and squared spindles. When grouped like a

delicate screen around a sturdy cantilevered table, Wright's tall-back dining chairs helped

EXPERIMENT, AND IS AS DELIGHTFULLY LIVABLE

form a room within each dining room (some had two), reinforcing on a smaller scale the

forms, materials, and colors of the overall space. Built-ins surrounded this central stage,

FOR SOME FAMILIES AS IT WOULD BE IMPOSSI-

which was often indirectly lighted from above and framed in art glass windows and

projecting bays to create the sensation of a golden prairie sunset. □ Wright's dining rooms

BLE FOR OTHERS." *HOUSE BEAUTIFUL*, JUNE 1905

remained formal even though the rest of his houses were becoming less constrained.

Each was so "coupled with the living room that one leads naturally into the other without

destroying the privacy of either," he said in 1901—although he had noted five years earlier

that he would have been happy if it were just a "sunny alcove" of the living room. To his

successful clients, however, dining was a conspicuous occasion for consumption. A formal

dining room also gave Wright the free rein he needed to paint a picture of family togeth-

erness, with members gathered upright in rectitude to honor the act of taking their meals.

From the intimate scale of the enclosed table, the Dana-Thomas
House dining room soars two stories to a ceiling whose color and
shape recall a ripe pumpkin. Behind butterfly chandeliers, a
mural featuring prairie sumac rings the room. At the Boynton
House of 1908 in Rochester, New York (pages 104–5), Wright
merged the dining room and breakfast nook in one grand space.

"Bowels, circulation, and nerves were new in buildings," Wright recalled in 1954, when the twentieth century took plumbing, steam heat, and electric lights for granted. In 1900 they were awkward new technologies to fit into a home as graciously as possible. Wright's answer was to build them in. ☐ "Naked" radiators were "an abomination," so the architect hid them behind tailor-made wood grilles to match his chairs and stair balusters. Placed near window ledges, their heat rose softly to warm the rooms. "Wright was quick to see," noted James Marston Fitch in the November 1955 *House Beautiful*, "that if all rooms could be kept equally comfortable with almost invisible heat sources, rooms could flow freely into one another." In the 1930s he began to build heat right into the floor. ☐ Bare hanging light fixtures were equally offensive. Wright welcomed this new invention of electric lights, however, and taught himself to paint rooms with this "beautifier" to illuminate them as never before. With indirect light, built into the warp and woof of a house, "spaces could be modeled, forms dramatized, textures enhanced," noted Fitch in the same *House Beautiful*. In addition to recessing artificial lights into ceiling fixtures, to filter out in jewel tones, Wright tucked them behind wood decks. These were projections of the bands that usually encircled his Prairie walls at the door-top and ceiling levels. From behind, the light sent diffused rays upward while outlining the precious objects grouped on the decks, which became yet another device for integrating art into the walls of a home.

"WRIGHT WENT BOLDLY AHEAD BUILDING THE UNADORNED BULB INTO THE VERY FABRIC OF HIS HOUSES. LIGHT ITSELF, AND NOT JUST THE FIXTURE, BECAME A SOURCE OF PLEASURE AND DELIGHT." JAMES MARSTON FITCH, *HOUSE BEAUTIFUL*, NOVEMBER 1955

Wright quickly became skilled at building light right into a room. At the May House of 1908 in Grand Rapids, Michigan, he placed lights behind wood decks at the window-top level so they could shine softly and indirectly upward. For a number of clients he even attached lamps to the corners of the dining table itself. Heat, in the form of radiators, did its work under the windows behind wood spindles like those used to screen views throughout the house.

"SONNETS IN STONE":

"IF HIS MESSAGE WAS SOMETIMES MISUNDER-

STOOD AND MISINTERPRETED, IT WAS BECAUSE

ARCHITECTURE HAD NEVER PREVIOUSLY BEEN

PRESENTED AS A MEDIUM FOR FREEING THE

INDIVIDUAL AND FOR PUTTING MAN INTO

PERSONAL, INTIMATE CONTACT WITH HIS

UNIVERSE." *HOUSE BEAUTIFUL*, OCTOBER 1959

FRANK LLOYD WRIGHT
AN AUTOBIOGRAPHY

The 1920s were a time of prosperity and high aspirations, but not for Wright. He had left his wife and family, closed his Oak Park studio, and lost the public acclaim of his Prairie years. High hopes turned to tragedy: his mistress was murdered, Taliesin burned twice, and Midway Gardens, his Chicago fantasia, went bankrupt in 1916, two years after it opened. At the beginning of the century's third decade, one of his few projects actually under construction was the majestic Imperial Hotel in Tokyo. It

1920S AND 1930S EXPERIMENTS

opened to the crescendo of the powerful Kanto earthquake of 1923. Wright's master-work stood firm, and so did its architect, who made a habit of rising, reborn, from disasters of all sorts. □ Wright became a composer in search of a new melody. He found one note in concrete—architecture's "gutter rat"—another in the primitive forms of pre-Columbian cultures, and a third in testing the limits of technology. In the early 1920s he began writing his new architectural themes in the Golden State. One exotic residence and four innovative houses in the Los Angeles area helped restore Wright's creative vision even if they did not bring in new clients. Soon the desert taught the artist from the Midwest how to build with the sun instead of for the snow. □ The American home remained Wright's focus, and he turned his attention to housing people of moderate means. But in the midst of this transformation, in 1935, Wright quickly sketched out a weekend house over a waterfall in Pennsylvania for the parents of one of his students. Added to the insights of his 1932 *Autobiography*, his daring terraced house in the trees for Edgar and Liliane Kaufmann, now known the world over as Fallingwater, restored Wright as an architectural force to be reckoned with.

DRAMATIC SITES

Wright left the prairie behind—in reality as well as in the imagination—as commissions

took him to Japan, the West, and the hills of Pennsylvania. Wherever he went, a good site

remained his first prescription. He liked difficult places to build, however—spots no one else

wanted. □ Of the four concrete-block houses built from 1923 to 1926 around Los Angeles,

La Miniatura rests in a ravine prone to flooding, the Storer House is tucked into a bend of

a road in the Hollywood Hills, the Freeman House is perched on the side of a hill, entered

from above, and the Ennis House clings to a steep ridge. Only Hollyhock House of 1917–21

stretches serenely across a crest in Hollywood. Fallingwater cascades into its valley like

the waterfall itself, affirming yet almost defying nature. In Racine, Wisconsin, the 1937 Wing-

spread "rides the grassy slopes of the shallow ravines," reported *House Beautiful* in

November 1955, "with the lightness and security of a sturdy ship on a calm, quiet sea."

□ Taliesin West, the architect's winter home after 1937 in Scottsdale, Arizona, adopted the

shape of the mountains as its design cue, the stones of the desert as its materials and color,

and the sun as its guiding light. Here Wright turned his familiar straight lines and flat planes

into what he called "dotted lines" reflecting the textures of sand and saguaros. □ The

warmer sites of the West and Southwest gave Wright more design freedom. Roofs became

less important as shelter and could even be turned into outdoor viewing platforms. Holly-

hock House's main rooms open onto a courtyard whose only roof is the sky. In summer Fall-

ingwater's terraces offer almost as much living space as the rooms inside. No one notices

that a site is beautiful, suggested Wright in 1939, until a beautiful house opens their eyes.

Wright let the site dictate his architectural response. Mountains and hills provided inspiration at Taliesin West (top left), his desert home in Scottsdale, Arizona, and at the Ennis House (top right) in Los Angeles. La Miniatura (bottom left) grew from a ravine in Pasadena, California, while Fallingwater (bottom right and pages 112–13) branched out like a tree over a Pennsylvania stream.

EXOTIC MOTIFS

Even as a boy, Wright recalled in *A Testament* in 1957, primitive American architecture built

by the Toltecs, Aztecs, Mayans, and Incas "stirred my wonder, excited my wishful admira-

"A POET WHO WROTE HIS SONNETS IN SYL-

tion." To him these earth buildings were great abstractions, masonry masses "planned as

one mountain." He had dipped into the palette of exoticism in the previous decade, begin-

LABLES OF STONE—THAT WAS FRANK LLOYD

ning with Taliesin and then Midway Gardens and the Imperial Hotel, and primitive motifs can

be found on works such as the German Warehouse of 1915–20 and the Bogk House of 1916,

WRIGHT." *HOUSE BEAUTIFUL*, OCTOBER 1959

both in Wisconsin. ☐ California in the 1920s seemed an inviting place to build abstract

mountains of his own. Hollyhock House, with its battered stucco walls and mystical friezes

In designs such as Hollyhock House, Wright rejected the austere
modern architecture bubbling up in Europe and seemed to align
himself instead with the modern artists who saw something simpler and more natural in the less developed cultures of the world.

(hollyhocks all), calls to mind a Mayan temple, circa 1921. Seeking an analogy in music,

Wright named it his "California Romanza," his ode to joy. Not far away, Charles and Mabel

Ennis's 1923 house reprised the Mayan motif in square-patterned concrete blocks raised

to build a fortress on their hill overlooking Los Angeles. □ Nature's own primitivism—

mountains, cacti, sun, shadow, and desert floor—provided the model for Taliesin West.

"There is a feeling of something almost prehistoric in the masonry which surrounds it,"

House Beautiful told readers in December 1946. "It lacks almost completely those familiar

identifying tags which allow us to label, classify, and evaluate."

NEW WAYS OF BUILDING

Wright was an innovator all his life, continually seeking new ways to stretch the possibilities of materials and especially to reduce costs by simplifying the construction process. In the 1920s and 1930s the middle-aged weaver took masonry, from lowly concrete to desert stones, as his warp and woof and knit together new building fabrics. □ Concrete was a "mud pie" to Wright, with "neither song nor any story," he said in 1928. Yet he used it in 1923

to fabricate four truly organic houses in California whose structure and ornament, inside and outside, were joined as one. Sixteen-inch blocks were cast on site in varying geometric

patterns "textured like the trees," setting the unit system for each house. Interwoven with steel, these "textile" blocks were just about everything Wright wanted: tough, light but not

thin, plastic, inexpensive, imperishable, and with the honest look of the machine. Standardization, which he had dreamed of for a 1906 residence, was finally his. □ At Fallingwater

Wright cantilevered broad terraces of concrete like "a tray on a waiter's fingers," observed John deKoven Hill in the November 1955 *House Beautiful.* The owner and contractor wanted

the security of more steel in the "trays," and they got some of it, but Wright did not get his wish to leaf them in gold. □ In Arizona the architect was his own client, and he followed the example

of the sturdy saguaro and the "rock-bound earth prostrate to the sun." His apprentices at Taliesin West rolled desert boulders into forms and filled them with concrete, on Wright's loom no longer an architectural outcast. Canvas roofs dotted wooden lines like cactus blossoms. The master, said *House Beautiful* in December 1946, "has designed not only with stone, wood, and canvas, but has used sun and shadow as though they, too, were materials."

With concrete-block designs such as the Freeman (top left) and Storer (top right) Houses in Los Angeles, Wright hoped to bring the factory to the home. He succeeded at Taliesin West (bottom left), where boulders were collected in 1937 to form mountainous walls. In 1929, for his cousin Richard Lloyd Jones of Tulsa, Oklahoma, he paired plain blocks with towers of glass (bottom right).

Freed from the flat line of the prairie, Wright began allowing his houses to soar. It was as if

he had forsaken the Prairie years' branching canopy of leaves for the upright trunk of the

tree. Before this time, and again toward the end of his life, he railed against the "empty

grandeur" of high ceilings designed to give residents an inferiority complex, to make them

feel insignificant. "When any ceiling is evident as low or lofty," Wright wrote in 1945, "then

something is gone wrong." ☐ In his four California concrete-block houses, lofty ceilings

inside mirror the vertical architectural thrust of stacked rooms outside. But Wright brought

"A SOARING ROOF CAN ELEVATE THE HEART;

their two-story lift down to human scale by weaving in various devices: a balcony off the

bedroom overlooking La Miniatura's living room and changing levels—steps up, steps down,

A VISTA OPENING TO SUNLIT SPACE OR TO

cross beams—in other rooms. Glass pierces the walls to frame the spectacular views of hills

and canyons that probably emboldened him to reach for the sky in the first place.

NATURE'S RESTFUL GREEN CAN RESTORE THE

☐ Although Wright complained that Americans loved to "Paul Bunyanize" things, the folk

hero would have found room to stretch himself in the three-story living area of Wingspread.

SPIRIT." *HOUSE BEAUTIFUL*, OCTOBER 1959

It was a tall space for what the architect considered his last Prairie house. People of

average height do not have to bend over to avoid the mezzanine that cuts across the

towering forest of skylights to offer a comforting branch of shelter (see pages 9 and 121).

Wright's reach in the garden room at Taliesin West was less Gargantuan yet more

pronounced. Inspired by the McDowell Mountains nearby, he canted his ceiling upward

from a low stone wall to form a right triangle. Decked out in their original wood-framed,

operable white canvas "sails," all the roofs soared upward, said Wright, "like ships coming

down the mesa . . . a new kind of desert fleet."

At La Miniatura, Wright's 1923 "textile" block house in Pasadena,
he helped Alice Millard, one of his earlier clients, find a new way
of living in her newly adopted state. Off a ground-floor terrace
he put the dining room and kitchen; above them the living room
rises block by block a full two stories. Viewed from the bedroom-
level balcony, Wright's generous gift of height becomes obvious.

119

It showed up in California, and in Arizona, just as it did in the frigid Midwest. The family fireplace remained at the heart of Wright's houses whether the temperature outside was frightful or delightful. Warmth was not the sole quality a good fireplace radiated for Wright. □ In the 1920s and 1930s his hearths became one with their houses, linked by materials and forms. The same concrete patterns and shapes that mark the California "textile" block residences stamp the character of the fireplaces. At Taliesin West in Arizona the fifteen fireplaces, like the house's walls, rise with cemented boulders into mountains as powerful as the ones behind Wright's desert refuge. Gnarled fingers of sandstone protrude from the waterfall to form Fallingwater's living room hearth. The openings, horizontal or sometimes vertical, remained cavelike, but the fireplaces tended to take over an entire wall. □ Wingspread's extraordinary fireplace, brick like the house's exterior, rises three stories to vanish into the "wigwam" ceiling. Five fire caves are carved out of its sculpted core, which is an indomitable wall of flame that apportions the immense living area into cozy nooks. Equally distinctive is Hollyhock House's fireplace, the focal point of the living room. An exotic, asymmetrical altar cast in modern concrete, its circles, diamonds, and rectilinear shapes tell the story of the house's geometry. An octagonal hearth floats in a golden pool, and lighted glass stands in for the sky. Earth, air, fire, and water—in this one spot Wright brought them all together.

"[WRIGHT] LAID BARE ONE OF THE MANY CONTRA-DICTORY ELEMENTS IN THE NATURE OF MAN: THE EMOTIONAL DESIRE FOR LIBERATING SPACE VS. THE PRIMITIVE NEED FOR SHELTER AND PRIVACY."

GUY HENLE, *HOUSE BEAUTIFUL*, OCTOBER 1959

Hollyhock House's concrete fireplace (top left) celebrates geometry as well as the four elements. At Wingspread (top right) the three-story brick chimney deftly divides the house's spacious living area. Fallingwater's rocky hearth (bottom left) was shaped naturally from boulders found right on the spot. Taliesin West's fireplaces (bottom right) mimic the rusticity of a desert camp.

In the early 1920s Wright was without the many "fingers" on his hands who had helped him

furnish his Prairie houses so compatibly. He was constantly in motion between Japan

and California and back to Wisconsin, with little time to attend to construction details,

much less furniture. And dining was becoming more informal—typically moved to a corner

of the living area—and thus less of an artistic challenge for him. Aline Barnsdall at Holly-

hock House nonetheless received a dining table and chairs as theatrical as she. Just as

stone hollyhocks rise along her walls to carve out the house's central motif, they climb the

chair backs in wood. Encircling the octagonal hearth in the living room is an all-in-one,

freestanding "built-in" providing seating, light, and table surfaces. Hands who guided this

work for Wright included his son Lloyd and the Austrian émigré Rudolph M. Schindler.

□ As lifestyles were simplified in the next decade, Wright returned to the furniture mainstay

of his early career: built-ins. Fallingwater, a weekend retreat meant to be carefree, was an

object lesson in how to tuck furniture into the architecture. From the forty-eight-foot-long

living room to the dining nook and kitchen and on into the bedrooms and guest rooms,

built-in sofas, tables, desks, cabinets, and bookcases streamlined living as they simplified

the design. Wright repeated the formula at Wingspread and Taliesin West, leaving a few

interesting pieces "at large." For his desert home he cleverly folded plywood (another

building industry orphan) into butterfly chairs whose wings seem poised for flight—

using the Japanese art of origami to make sitters look graceful in spite of themselves.

"WRIGHT PROVED THAT THE ELEMENTS IN A BUILDING, LIKE ORCHESTRATION IN GREAT MUSIC, CAN BE MADE POWERFUL CONTRIBUTORS, EACH IN ITS OWN WAY, TO THE BEAUTY OF THE TOTAL ENVIRONMENT." *HOUSE BEAUTIFUL*, OCTOBER 1959

Like much of Wright's later furniture, the pieces in Taliesin West's garden room (top) and cabaret theater (bottom) were made of plain materials such as plywood and designed to be moved around to create new conversation clusters. Geometric shapes and natural colors of the desert prevailed here. At Fallingwater (pages 124–25) built-in sofas, tables, and footstools cantilever outward in imitation of the house's famous terraces. Like autumn leaves fallen to the ground, the cushions accent the stone-colored upholstery.

"ENDLESS VARIATIONS UP HIS SLEEVE":

"THE HOUSE IS ALL STRAIGHT LINES AND

RIGHT ANGLES—ON THE BLUEPRINTS. IN THE

FLESH IT IS LIKE A GENTLY MOLDED GIRL

WHO CARRIES HERSELF ERECTLY." LOREN

POPE, *HOUSE BEAUTIFUL*, AUGUST 1948

As much as life at home was changing in the mid-1930s, Wright feared that his organic architecture had no future without an organic society to match. So he pushed his clients to learn how to live a simpler life in Usonia—his term for a reinvigorated United States of North America. He redoubled his efforts to design "the house of moderate cost," which to Wright was "not only America's major architectural problem but the problem most difficult for her major architects." ☐ Beginning with the first of two

HOUSES FOR THE NEW AMERICA houses designed for

Herbert and Katherine Jacobs of Madison, Wisconsin, in 1936 and continuing for the two decades left to him, Wright created about 140 varied houses that helped change the shape of the single-family home. Not a new style, Usonians were a new way of building for a new type of client: one usually on a limited budget. All unnecessary complications of construction and living were discarded. Standardized materials saved time and money, and sandwich walls made inside and outside identical. Flat, overhanging roofs married the building to the earth just as Wright had made his Prairie houses companions to the horizon. Wide-open living areas—the dining table set into an alcove, near the kitchen—embraced a garden terrace on the house's private side. ☐ These not-so-big houses on small suburban lots liberated residents through spaciousness and vistas. It was mostly these models for modern living that *House Beautiful* shared with readers in its 1940s and 1950s features on Wright. At the same time he was also exploring multiple-family Usonian dwellings, prefabricated and do-it-yourself homes, cooperative communities, and an idealized plan for America's residential future called Broadacre City. Each of his Usonian houses, said Wright in 1954, was meant to instill "the new sense of space, light, and freedom—to which our U.S.A. is entitled."

PREFAB EFFICIENCY

Houses cost too much, Wright might have said. To save time and money, he spent much of

his career trying to find ways to simplify not just the look of his buildings but how they

were constructed as well. During 1915–17 he designed "ready-cut" components for a

Milwaukee company, American System-Built Houses, to fabricate in a factory for assembly

on site. His 1920s concrete-block houses in Los Angeles were meant to streamline the

"HE FELT IN BEETHOVEN'S SYMPHONIES AND QUAR-

process even further. But it was with the Usonians that Wright finally thought he could

bring the factory to the home. □ His goals were to eliminate as much on-site labor as

TETS AN ARCHITECTURAL QUALITY. . . . BEETHOVEN

possible and to build the Usonian house outside and inside in a single step. To do so Wright

expanded the grid planning that underlay his Prairie houses, using a vertical module sized

BUILT AN EDIFICE IN WHICH NOTHING WAS SUPER-

at one foot, one inch and a two-by-four-foot horizontal unit system based on materials

such as plywood. This produced a framework akin to a cage in which everything would fit

FLUOUS, NOTHING MERELY PRETTY, NOTHING ADDED

uniformly, with no surprises, "like tapestry—a consistent fabric woven of interdependent,

related units," explained the weaver in 1957. □ Walls for the typical 1,500-square-foot, early

AS MEANINGLESS DECORATION. . . ." RICHARD

Usonian were designed to be factory made and shipped in sections for assembly on site,

roof first, often supervised by one of Wright's apprentices. Heating, lighting, and plumbing

WILLIAMS, *HOUSE BEAUTIFUL*, NOVEMBER 1955

systems were consolidated for easy installation. □ Estimated to cost $5,500 to $8,000,

many of these "assembled houses" ended up exceeding the budget, so some clients became

their own contractors or builders. Wright also tried self-build and prefabricated houses,

teaming up with the Marshall Erdman Company in the mid-1950s on twenty prefabs, but

these, too, broke the bank—although not his desire to build the perfect home of moderate cost.

The board-and-batten siding chosen for the first Jacobs House of 1936 in Madison, Wisconsin, fit perfectly into Wright's uniform planning grid. He also experimented again with concrete blocks in designs he called Usonian Automatics—houses intended to practically build themselves. The Tonkens House of 1954 outside Cincinnati (pages 130–31) became one of the most luxurious.

Despite the straitened times of the Great Depression, the material shortages of World

War II, and rising construction costs fueled by postwar prosperity, Wright still wanted to put

American families in affordable homes of their own. Paring down, he narrowed his stock of

materials to five—wood, brick, concrete, paper, and glass (with steel for cantilevers and a

few stones occasionally thrown in)—and let them dictate the spare forms of his new houses.

□ In the earliest, prewar Usonians, the walls outside and in were usually board and batten,

"THE MATERIALS OF BUILDING ARE TO THE CRE-

built of three thicknesses of boards with insulation paper between them, all fastened with

screws. To Wright this sandwich construction was a kind of plywood on a grand scale. Pine

ATIVE ARCHITECT WHAT WORDS ARE TO THE POET.

with redwood battens gave the first Jacobs House of 1936 its own built-in color and pattern;

for clients with more to spend, cypress replaced pine, even turning ceilings into woodsy

BUT MATERIALS, AS WORDS, MUST EXPRESS THEIR

forests. □ Brick linked the houses to the earth from the chimney stack down through foun-

dations and terraces. Like wood, which Wright always thought the most "humanly intimate of

TRUE MEANING TO BE BEAUTIFUL AND REAL."

all materials," brick also came indoors to build fireplaces and walls as rosy as Wright's red

cement floors. And everywhere, glass brought light inside to beautify each home. Later

ROBERT MOSHER, *HOUSE BEAUTIFUL*, NOVEMBER 1955

Usonians were clad in rough-laid stone, concrete block (patterned or plain), or simple rein-

forced concrete in combination with wood. □ To simplify the budget, not to mention the

architecture, Wright eliminated the plasterer and the painter along with visible roofs, gutters,

and downspouts; basements; and interior extravagances such as ornamental trim. In the

spirit of democracy, it was "honest" construction designed to set the individual free—integral

to its site, its materials, and the life of its inhabitants.

Up to his last house, concrete remained a staple of Wright's building palette. For the Adelman House of 1946 in Fox Point, Wisconsin, stepped, buff-toned blocks sheath the exterior (top) and line interior walls as well. Cypress adds a softening touch in features such as built-in storage cabinets in a hallway (bottom left) and creates, as the November 1955 *House Beautiful* noted, a "structural rhythm" in the house's ceiling framing (bottom right).

INFORMAL LIVING

Out went the dining room, replaced by a dining alcove. In came a "workspace" in lieu of a big kitchen run by hired help. Down came the bedrooms from the second story. And the living area, open to nature like a garden conservatory, took over nearly half of the floor space. Wright's standard Usonian, "a thing loving the ground," completed the domestic revolution begun in his Prairie houses. ☐ He ushered owners into active (living area) and quiet (bedroom) zones to simplify their lives. The informal three-part spatial arrangement—living and dining area, workspace with utilities, and bedrooms and baths reached by a "gallery" (hallway)—remained consistent even though his Usonians took many forms. The basic plan was L shaped, sometimes closed to 60 degrees or opened to 120 degrees to abolish the right angle. Others were in a straight line or a T, while more exotic modules drew on parallelograms, hexagons, triangles, ellipses, and circles. ☐ "It is like an iceberg, in that there is so much more than meets the eye," said Paul and Jean Hanna about their home in the January 1963 *House Beautiful.* The ever-important fireplace, now asymmetrical, led the eye to vistas beyond. Flowing spaces invited one "to go on and around corners," noted the Hannas, adding that their living room seemed visually larger than it was because no partitions declared that "here the room stops." Changing ceiling heights and floor levels added drama. Within these compact quarters lay a satisfying sense of freedom. "The occupant is always the center, always a participant and not an onlooker," Curtis Besinger observed in the same *House Beautiful.* Reflected Wright himself in his 1943 *Autobiography:* "I think a cultured American, we say Usonian, housewife will look well in it."

> "THE CHANGING LEVELS OR PLANES . . . AND THE DELICATE OPENNESS OF THE HOUSE GIVE THE SAME SENSE OF RELEASE AND SHELTER AS WALKING IN A FOREST, WHERE THE LEAFY LIMBS CUT SUNLIGHT AND SPACE INTO A CONTINUING SUCCESSION OF MYSTERIES."
> — LOREN POPE, *HOUSE BEAUTIFUL,* AUGUST 1948

In their 1936 house in Stanford, California, the Hannas could see three fireplaces from their bedroom. The couple told readers of the January 1963 *House Beautiful* that "the flames leap six feet high" in the sunken living room hearth. At the 1945 Cedar Rock in Quasqueton, Iowa (pages 136–37), a skylight turns the indoors into a garden. The pierced ceiling bathes a built-in planter with light.

WINDOW WALLS

Glass and light are merely "two forms of the same thing," said Wright in 1928. With these

crystal-thin sheets of "air in air," he finally demolished the confining walls of a house and

invited nature right indoors. Floor-to-ceiling doors and clerestory eyebrows at ceiling

height almost fooled clients into thinking that they were living in a garden; in fact, Wright

"CUT BRANCHES OF TREES AND SHRUBS ARE ALWAYS

liked to view many of his later living areas as garden rooms. □ A Usonian's public face to

the street was relatively eyeless, but on the private side it opened with a glazed smile to

BEING TUCKED OVERHEAD, BELOW CLERESTORY

catch the southern sun. Glass was sized in modules like the other building materials, and

in some cases it was set in wood mullions that continued the line of the boards and battens

WINDOWS. THEY MERGE WITH THE FOLIAGE AND

or other units of the building system. French doors, shaded by the roof overhang, folded in

and out to nature like Wright's screens of old. The ceiling, meeting glass and continuing

BRANCHES SEEN THROUGH THESE HIGH WINDOWS,

outside via the roof overhang, effectively ran past the wall. Windows mitered at corners

made walls completely vanish. Clerestory bands at the point where walls met ceiling found

GIVING YOU THE FEELING THAT YOU ARE NOT REALLY

a natural spot to coax in views of sky and trees and to offer cross-ventilation; roofs

seemed to float above just as the Prairie houses were released by art glass friezes. Light

INDOORS." *HOUSE BEAUTIFUL*, NOVEMBER 1955

and air thus came not from holes punched in a box but through the house's framework

itself. □ Wright took his sun catching a step further with a number of "solar hemicycle"

houses such as those for the Jacobs (1944), Laurent (1949), and Rayward (1955) families.

Energy-conscious designs before anyone knew there was an energy crisis, these houses

abandoned right angles for an elliptical window wall to passively capture the sun's rays.

Wright knew how to use glass, said Joseph Barry in *House Beautiful's* November 1955

special issue, "to remove corners from our spirit as from our homes."

In the second house he designed for the Jacobs family, Wright
gave them a curving wall of glass to catch the sun—he called it
a "solar hemicycle." On the public side of their Wisconsin home,
a protective berm wraps the rough stone walls like a warm collar.

Wright's fascination with new technology continued inside from floor to ceiling. First he got

rid of visually intrusive radiators by placing heat in the floor. The idea came to him in

Japan in 1914 as he dined in a patron's "Korean room." Warm feet, cool head, he reasoned.

Coiled wrought-iron (later copper) pipes to carry hot water were set in a bed of crushed

rock and covered with a thin concrete "floormat." Stained red, waxed, and inscribed with

the geometric module of the house, these floors gave Usonian houses a rich sheen while

warmth rose naturally as if from earthy clay. Using gravity heat, Wright was able to create

his own climate. (For clients who felt cold, he suggested warmer clothing. And for the

summer he preferred natural ventilation over artificial air conditioning.) ☐ Light was as

hidden as heat so that it seemed to emerge from the building itself. Wood decks about two

feet wide concealed fixtures as they encircled rooms to tie one space to another. It was a

combination made in heaven: indirect light reflecting off the ceiling and a ledge on which

to drape natural bouquets and family heirlooms like "incidental chords of music," as the

November 1955 *House Beautiful* called them. Where they met the roof overhang at a thin

glass wall, these decks also helped merge the inside with the outside. ☐ Closets had always

been "unsanitary boxes"—wasted rooms—to Wright. In his Usonians he turned hallways into

storage walls and lined some with bookcases. Even though already narrow, they became

efficient spaces with a character of their own. Each of these innovations stemmed from

Wright's desire to ensure that everything was harmonious and that nothing was out of place.

"WRIGHT WAS ONE OF OUR FIRST ARCHITECTS TO USE [GRAVITY]-HEATED CONCRETE FLOOR SLABS IN HIS HOUSES—A TECHNIQUE WHICH FREED HIS FLOORS OF RADIATORS AND REGISTERS. TO OFF-SET THEIR HARDNESS, HE SOMETIMES USES LUSH AREAS OF CARPETING. . . ." JAMES MARSTON FITCH, *HOUSE BEAUTIFUL*, NOVEMBER 1955

At the Adelman House in Fox Point, Wisconsin, Wright continued his practice of hiding lights in wood decks (top left) and building storage into walls (top right). A hallway at the Palmer House of 1950 in Ann Arbor, Michigan (bottom left), doubles as space for books; underneath the red concrete floor lie the gravity heating coils. A forced-air system was used for Crimson Beech, a 1957 Erdman prefab on Staten Island (bottom right). In the Usonians, a fireplace, often asymmetrical, added psychological warmth.

WORKSPACE KITCHENS

"This is your laboratory," Wright told Paul and Jean Hanna. "You should find it attractive

enough to be happy in." *House Beautiful* readers learned first-hand in January 1963 about

the evolution of the modern kitchen in Usonian homes such as the Hannas' hexagonal tour

de force in California. □ By today's standards, Wright's Usonian workspaces (his preferred

term) were small, not much larger than a ship's galley, but they represented a sea change

for women. No longer relegated to the back of the house, the kitchen took center stage in

the masonry core near the juncture of the living and dining areas. And Wright proclaimed

the housewife no longer "a kitchen-mechanic behind closed doors" but "the central figure

in her menage"—a gracious hostess who did not miss anything going on around her.

Cooking took place out of sight but close enough for her to watch over family and guests.

□ Finished in the same materials as the living spaces to achieve continuity, Usonian kitchens

variously had limited outside views or none. Those without windows, among them the

Hannas', rose high for ventilation and to pull in light from a clerestory or skylight. Glowing like

an inner court, the workspace's walls were freed for storage. Countertops and appliances

were never more than a few steps away, and open shelves held everyday items. Pass-

throughs (closable when not needed) allowed the hostess to borrow light and air from the

dining area. The workspace may have been too small for some clients and lacking in

windows, children may have gotten underfoot, and it was, after all, still a woman's preserve,

but at least, suggested James Marston Fitch in the November 1955 *House Beautiful*, the

homemaker was no longer "exiled from the rest of the family."

"THE KITCHEN IS SMALL AND COMPACT AND EVERY-
THING IS AT HAND. A MEAL CAN BE PREPARED AND
THE DISHES WASHED AND PUT AWAY—AND THE
CLOTHES WASHED IN THE BENDIX—ALMOST WITH-
OUT TAKING A STEP. AND WHILE MOTHER IS BUSY
IN HERE, SHE CAN SEE THROUGH THE HOUSE, OUT
INTO THE YARD WHERE THE CHILDREN PLAY."
LOREN POPE, *HOUSE BEAUTIFUL*, AUGUST 1948

The Stromquist House of 1958 in Bountiful, Utah, offers the illusion of a window in the kitchen—but it opens only onto the entry hall. Its ceiling rises high to inject a sense of spaciousness into the compact workspace. Concrete and wood, including the perforated window screen and a deck encircling the room, seamlessly carry through the materials used in the rest of the house.

Just as Wright's geometric art glass became a signature of his Prairie-style houses, perfo-

rated wood cutouts characterized his Usonians. Intricate art glass was well beyond a

teacher's salary, but screens punched out with fret-sawn geometric patterns could simi-

larly focus views and light for less cost. Wright turned cutouts into lacy shutters for

windows outside, ran them along ceiling-high clerestories, and made them into interior

screens that cast delightful patterns on walls and floors. □ From his earliest spindled

"MR. WRIGHT . . . JOYFULLY SHAKES ENDLESS

banisters and tall-back chairs, he had been fascinated by the shadow game played by

screens, comparing them to tree branches filtering light. For his Usonian houses, Wright let

VARIATIONS OUT OF HIS SLEEVE LIKE A MAGI-

each sing its own song in perforated wood patterns that related to the plan of the house

or featured a unique geometric motif. Cutout boards, usually plywood, were combined this

CIAN PERFORMING CARD TRICKS." ELIZABETH

way and that to form decorative variations. □ Some of Wright's most distinctive patterns

can be found at the Pope-Leighey House of 1939 in Mount Vernon, Virginia, where a vaguely

GORDON, *HOUSE BEAUTIFUL*, NOVEMBER 1955

turtlelike creature shields the end bedroom windows, crawls along the hall, and marches

up and around the living area (the turtle may actually be the hexagonal plan of the Hanna

House). At the Smith House in Bloomfield Hills, Michigan, begun in 1946, a cutout screen

over the dining table recalls the fret-sawn light cover Wright used to bring "moonlight" into

his own Oak Park dining room in 1895. Good ideas were worth recycling, especially if they

could be inexpensively woven right into the fabric of these moderate-cost residences.

Cutout wood panels placed over side and clerestory windows
usher light into the Pope-Leighey House of 1939 in Mount Vernon,
Virginia, sprinkling patterns on the incised red floor of its living
area. Describing "The Love Affair of a Man and His House" in the
August 1948 *House Beautiful,* Loren Pope explained to readers
that "the clerestory windows at ceiling level carry off the hot air,
and the layout of the openings in the house creates a breeze."

MODULAR FURNISHINGS

Before minimalism was in, there were Usonian interiors. For the sake of simplicity and efficiency, all toward the goal of "more gracious living," Wright tried to remove everything he could: from radiators, light fixtures, paint, plaster, and trim to most freestanding furniture, pictures, and the dust-catching bric-a-brac that had hounded him since the 1890s.

Usonian walls (and floors) were made to include these traditional household accoutrements, or, as he urged, to actually *be* them. □ Furniture was simple, often designed to be made of plywood on site, and built in or destined for double duty. Sofas were attached to walls, as were dining tables (some in sections) to free up the center space and make narrow rooms look wider. Open shelves served variously as room dividers and as roosts for books and carefully arranged decorative objects. Geometric footstools and tables moved around as needed. Comfortable chairs likewise were light enough to carry. Bedrooms had custom beds as well as dressers that could also serve as desks. Although simple, each piece was a part of the whole, created to form and reform new combinations while reinforcing the rectangular, triangular, hexagonal, or circular geometry of the house itself. □ To go with the usual waxed red floor, nubby weaves in warm reds, rusts, golds, and tans were often used for upholstered seats and cushions. Natural-hued carpeting was cut to underscore the house's grid, with room sometimes left for oriental rugs as accents. And for the decidedly cozy living area of the Pope-Leighey House and many others, Wright even sketched in a grand piano, a sign perhaps of his grand ambitions for these modest dwellings.

"HE WOULD COME INTO A ROOM AND SEE IMMEDIATELY WHAT SHOULD BE MOVED TO CREATE A MORE PLEASING ARRANGEMENT. HE ALSO CREATED COMPOSITIONS OF SMALL OBJECTS AND FLOWERS THAT HE CALLED 'EYE MUSIC.'" JOHN DeKOVEN HILL, *HOUSE BEAUTIFUL*, JUNE 1992

From the entrance gate on inside, triangles set the theme for the Ablin House of 1958 in Bakersfield, California (top), down to the pomegranate-colored Philippine mahogany furniture made from Wright's designs. Tables and chairs in the glassed-in dining area of Auldbrass, Wright's 1939 plantation in Yemassee, South Carolina (bottom), pick up the house's hexagonal motif, while built-in seating in the Laurent House of 1949 in Rockford, Illinois (pages 148–49), mirrors the elliptical flow of its windows.

In her attention-getting April 1953 editorial, Elizabeth Gordon, *House Beautiful's* editor,

proclaimed Bauhaus furniture "sterile, cold, thin, uncomfortable." She soon found a solution:

have Wright design furnishings affordable even to people who did not own one of his

houses. The eighty-six-year-old architect had always insisted on the uniqueness of each of

his designs—writing in 1954 that "every chair must eventually be designed for the building

it is to be used in"—yet he had long admired the potential of machine technology. If mass

production could extend his principles to a new audience, and not incidentally produce

needed royalties, Wright saw its value in a new light. □ Gordon first persuaded F. Schu-

"AND NOW FRANK LLOYD WRIGHT DESIGNS

macher and Company to develop a line of fabrics and wallpapers (the latter was some-

thing Wright had previously criticized). Wright motifs were adapted and new designs

HOME FURNISHINGS YOU CAN BUY!"

created based on his architectural plans. "Everything had to go together," stressed *House*

Beautiful in announcing Wright's Taliesin Line in November 1955. □ That special issue on

HOUSE BEAUTIFUL, NOVEMBER 1955

Wright also featured modular geometric furniture made to his designs by Heritage-

Henredon. Hexagonal tables that could be assembled like Froebel blocks, footstools that

tucked into sofas, round tables, expandable sideboards, movable bookcases, and an inge-

nious desk—whether in circles, squares, or triangles, all were meant "to group and regroup

. . . to meet the many situations demanded by today's living room," noted *House Beautiful*. All

were coordinated with the fabrics and wallpapers as well as thirty-six paint colors from

Cherokee Red to Spring Green offered by the Martin Senour Company. Karastan's planned

carpets were never produced, but several of the 1955 lines have been reissued as part of

the array of Wright reproductions and adaptations that now bring the Wright style home.

With its crisp lines, Wright's Heritage-Henredon furniture fit well
into the Tonkens home in Ohio. Slant-back chairs filled the dining
nook, and hexagonal nesting tables held center stage in the living room. Ottomans were upholstered in a Schumacher brocade.

Wright wanted to give his Usonian homeowners as much garden as money allowed. The great outdoors became one of the most important "rooms" in these compact houses. Paul and Jean Hanna's 1936 Honeycomb House in Stanford, California, had so many windows and doors that the couple had "a perpetual ringside seat at the great performances of nature, from sunrises to thunder storms," they told *House Beautiful* readers in January 1963. □ Usonian patios often snuggled into the sunny, glass-lined ell at the back side of the house, hidden away from the public facade. Terraces, an integral part of the house grid, might extend from the living to the sleeping areas. Planter boxes outside windows brought nature to eye level while they linked a house to the land. Distant trees and hills became part of the landscape plan. Fruit trees and shrubs that grew fast enough to give up boughs were favorites; displayed inside, they offered a living link with nature. In the desert, Wright liked a refreshing fountain for its sound and rainbow spray (the Hannas were awakened by a clock activated by their garden waterfall). Maintenance was meant to be low cost and relatively carefree. □ Wright's Usonian houses helped reacquaint Americans with their own backyards. As Curtis Besinger described the Hanna House in *House Beautiful* in January 1963, each was "essentially a roof poised lightly" above a terrace, an abstraction of trees. "As a space," he wrote, "the house provides sensations similar to those you might experience within the open, yet protective, shelter of the great oak trees." The Hannas themselves reported that they were "still discovering new places to go out to. . . . Like the rooms of the house itself, these outdoor areas and segments of areas defy conventional nomenclature."

"THE OUTDOORS IS SO ADROITLY MADE A PART OF THE LIVING SCHEME THAT THE DWELLER BREATHES AS DEEPLY AS IN A MEADOW IN SPRING."

LOREN POPE, *HOUSE BEAUTIFUL*, AUGUST 1948

California sunlight weaves shadows into the hexagonal floor of the Hannas' outdoor rooms. Shade prevails in the concrete-block atrium of Wright's 1954 house for Marylou and Harold Price Sr. in Paradise Valley, Arizona (pages 154–55). Open to the desert and sky, cooled by a fountain, and warmed by a fireplace, it "creates its own climate," said the November 1956 *House Beautiful.*

Wright, a lover of fast cars, started his seventy-two-year career in the horse-and-buggy age and ended it in the age of the Impala. He began by designing stables, graduated to garages, and finally gave homeowners a new place to park their cars: under a carport, one of a number of domestic conveniences he nudged into existence. □ By the early 1900s Wright was housing his clients' newfangled automobiles in their own garages, although in August 1911 *House Beautiful* chose to cite one of the architect's earlier designs: the "clever combination stable and garage" in which he and William Winslow began printing their book *The House Beautiful* in 1896. In his feature "Housing the Automobile," Charles White commended the two wings that kept the equine ammonia from tarnishing the cars but also

"THERE WILL NEVER BE ANOTHER GARAGE FOR US."

boldly predicted that there "isn't much left to perfect in the motor car." Wright himself perfected detached garages, basement parking areas, and then, with the Robie House of

LOREN POPE, *HOUSE BEAUTIFUL*, AUGUST 1948

1908, the attached three-car garage. □ But he became tired of a garage's usual "gaping hole," making the leap to a carport in the early 1930s. Wright took issue with the "livery-stable mind" of Detroit ("It believes that the car is a horse and must be stabled"), countering in his 1943 *Autobiography:* "A carport will do, with liberal overhead shelter and walls on two sides." The cantilevered porte cochere of his early years became an off-street port for "the now inevitable car," which to Wright was a symbol of freedom: rolling access to nature, an easy getaway from the city. A carport saved his clients the cost of a garage and guaranteed that the modern age's new necessity would become an integral part of a house's design.

One observer called Wright's carports "a great bird in flight." The space-age design at the Friedman House of 1948 in Pleasantville, New York (top)—easily accommodating three- and four-wheeled vehicles alike—is a punctuation mark on the house itself: two circular stone towers. Perched above the Wapsipinicon River in Iowa, Cedar Rock (bottom) shelters its car under a swath of concrete that sweeps inland from the bluff. John deKoven Hill supervised the house's construction before he went to *House Beautiful.*

ROOM FOR EXPANSION

Families keep expanding, joked Wright in 1954, so "their architect has to tuck the extra chil-

dren in somehow." He did not want to "put them into little cells, double-decker them, and

shove them off into the tail of the house where life becomes one certain round of washing

diapers"—nothing could be further from his ideal of the harmony and serenity needed to

cushion a child's growth. Better than the traditional "box" of a home, Usonians were "an

ideal breeding stable." ☐ Wright built them to change, to either add or subtract children or

"SELDOM HAS A HOUSE BEEN MORE PUSHED ABOUT AND

activities. Organic architecture was meant to be a dynamic process, so any organic

building could continue to grow. He even called his Usonian houses "polliwogs": tadpoles

REWORKED FOR CHANGING NEEDS THAN OURS." PAUL

with a short or long tail. The tail—the bedroom wing—could expand or metamorphose as

needed, curving "like a centipede" if it got too long. ☐ The 1939 Rosenbaum House in

AND JEAN HANNA, *HOUSE BEAUTIFUL*, JANUARY 1963

Florence, Alabama, was the first Usonian to be enlarged, ten years after its construction,

with a courtyard addition designed by Wright. Paul and Jean Hanna undertook their 1936

California hexagon with the express wish to change "any detail we wished whenever we

wished," they told *House Beautiful* in January 1963. Screenlike, non-weight-bearing walls

dividing their children's bedrooms came down easily in 1957 to form a new master suite.

Board-and-batten walls and the unit construction of all the Usonians facilitated such

alterations. ☐ This was all as it should be to Wright, who said in his 1932 *Autobiography:*

"Take comfort in the thought that architecture, too, is a flux, a rapidly changeable working

of principle in the world's workshop—manifest in one form today, tomorrow in another."

Both the Hanna House (opposite) and the Smith House of 1946 in Bloomfield Hills, Michigan (below), were designed to grow organically. The Hannas got a "Fallingwater" fountain, while in 1969 the Smiths extended their house's "polliwog tail," its bedroom zone.

WRIGHT AT HOME

"JUST AS MR. WRIGHT'S ARCHITECTURE IS A

PERSONAL CHOICE FOR ONE'S OWN HOME, SO,

OBVIOUSLY IS HIS FURNITURE. THEY BOTH ARE

WRIGHTIAN—AND THAT IS SAYING A GREAT

DEAL." *HOUSE BEAUTIFUL*, NOVEMBER 1955

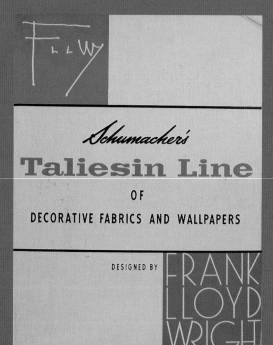

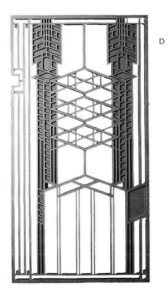

CIRCLE-IN-SQUARE PLANTER (A)

Cast sandstone. 30″ square, 20″ high. Nichols Bros. Stoneworks. Robie® House urn. Circle-in-square planters were one of Wright's Prairie-style signatures. This is usable indoors as well as outdoors.

SPRITE SCULPTURES (B)

Cast stone. 15″ high. Omnia/Alva. Reproductions of two of Alfonso Iannelli's sculptures from Midway Gardens (1913) in Chicago, intended for indoor use, capture the site's geometric forms.

HOLLYHOCK URN (C)

Cast crushed marble. 20″ wide, 8 ¾″ deep, 12″ high. Omnia. Recalling the stylized floral motifs used at Hollyhock House (1917–21), this versatile planter features a crest of abstract hollyhocks.

ROBIE GATE PANEL (D)

Hand-cast aluminum with oxidized metal finish. 28″ high, 16 ½″ wide. Historical Arts and Casting. A panel inspired by a courtyard gate of the Robie House (1908) works as a trellis or a wall ornament.

MOORE STEPPING STONES (E)

Cast stone. 10″ square, 1″ thick. Nichols Bros. Stoneworks. The design of these garden or walkway pavers comes from a wooden fretwork doorway in Wright's Moore House (1895, 1923) in Oak Park.

MAY HOUSE DESK (A)

Cherry, with walnut or black stain. 35" high, 45 1/4" wide, 24 1/2" deep. Cassina. This two-drawer desk with a shelf, designed with George Niedecken in 1908, mirrors the horizontal line of the prairie.

BARREL CHAIR (B)

Cherry, in natural or walnut or black stain. 31 3/4" high, 21 1/2" wide, 21 7/8" deep. Cassina. Designed for the Darwin Martin House (1904), this famous chair was one Wright remade for Wingspread in 1937.

TALL-BACK CHAIR (C)

Cherry, in natural or walnut stain. 52 1/2" high, 15 3/4" wide, 18" deep. Cassina. Robie® 1 Chair. Placed around the Robie House table, spindled chairs like these formed their own room within the room.

FRIEDMAN ARMCHAIR (D)

Cherry, with walnut or black stain. 28 1/2" high, 28 7/8" wide, 27 1/2" deep, with an ottoman. Cassina. A spindled back meets curved arms in this chair used at several of Wright's houses in the 1950s.

ROBIE SOFA (E)

Cherry, with walnut or black stain. 29 7/8" high, 94" wide, 40" deep. Cassina. Robie® 3 Sofa. The cantilevered arms and back reflect the sweep of the prairie, the "line of domesticity" for Wright.

IMPERIAL TOKYO CHAIR (F)

Fabric or leather upholstery, with cherry or walnut- or black-stained base. 29 1/2" high, 37 1/2" wide, 36 1/8" deep. Cassina. This streamlined chair and its twin sofa were used in the Imperial Hotel (1916–23).

TALIESIN TABLE (G)

Cherry, with walnut or black stain. 27 1/2" high, 75 1/2" or 98 1/2" long, 38 1/2" wide. Cassina. Taliesin® 2 Table. In 1925 Wright designed this table with spindled ends for Taliesin (1911), where it can still be seen.

PRAIRIE DINING SET (H)

Cherry, with walnut or black stain. Various sizes. Cassina. Husser Table and Coonley I Chair. Low-back spindled Coonley chairs pair up with a cantilevered Husser table whose ends are also spindled.

CANTILEVERED COFFEE TABLES (I)

Cherry, with walnut or black stain. 35 1/2" or 45 1/4" square, 16 1/8" high. Cassina. In Wright's 1939 design for his friend Lloyd Lewis, the table top appears to float over a raised shelf and inset slat legs.

MIDWAY METAL CHAIR AND TABLE (J)

Steel enameled in white, red, blue, or gray. Chair 34 1/2" high, 15 3/4" wide, 18 1/8" deep. Table 47 1/4" round or square. Cassina. Midway® 2 Chair and Midway® 3 Table. Circles and cascading triangles reinforce the leitmotif of Chicago's Midway Gardens complex.

A

B

C

D

E

F

C

H

I

J

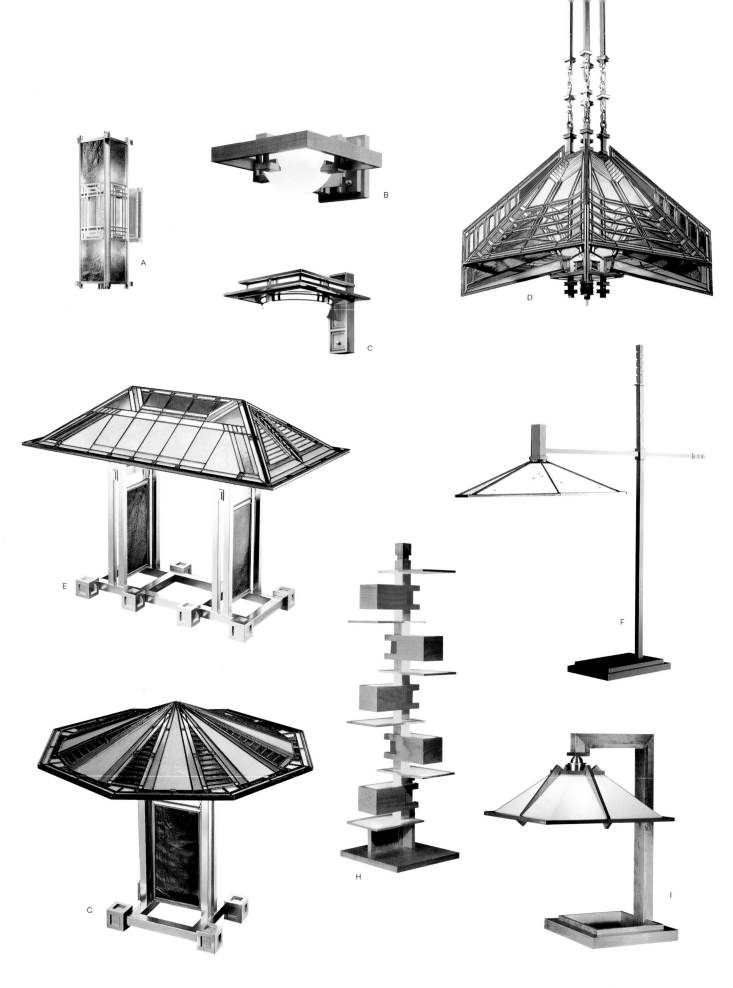

A

B

C

D

E

C

F

H

I

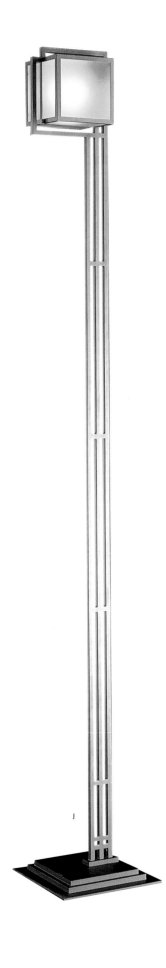

SUMAC WALL SCONCE (A)

Polished brass and iridescent glass. 13 ³⁄₈" high, 3 ³⁄₄" wide, 5" deep. Yamagiwa. Sumac® 4 Sconce. The rectilinear patterns Wright used in his art glass were designed to be easily fabricated.

CHERRY WALL SCONCE (B)

Cherry and frosted glass. 7" high, 11¼" wide, 13⅛" deep. Yamagiwa. Robie® 1 Sconce. A globe of soft light appears to float out from the wall, held in place only by a band of wood encircling it at midpoint.

ROBIE WALL SCONCE (C)

Antique brass and frosted glass. 7⅛" high, 8⅞" wide, 11" deep. Yamagiwa. Robie® 2 Sconce. A half-moon globe hangs from a top plate perforated with abstract fern designs visible above and below.

BUTTERFLY CHANDELIER (D)

Brass and iridescent glass. 22" high, 23¼" wide and deep. Yamagiwa. Sumac® 1 Lamp. Mimicking fluttering butterflies on the prairie, hanging lamps like these light the Dana-Thomas House (1902) table.

DOUBLE-PEDESTAL LAMP (E)

Brass and iridescent glass. 23¼" high, 32½" wide, 19¼" deep. Yamagiwa. Sumac® 3 Lamp. Prairie sumac inspired this lamp and other lighting fixtures in Susan Lawrence Dana's sumptuous home.

MIDWAY TABLE LAMP (F)

Painted steel and opal glass. 30³⁄₈" high, 13³⁄₄" wide, 29½" deep. Yamagiwa. Delicately suspended metal lamps such as these sat on the festive dining tables at Wright's Midway Gardens in Chicago.

IRIDESCENT UMBRELLA LAMP (G)

Brass and iridescent glass. 22⅝" high, 27³⁄₄" wide and deep. Yamagiwa. Sumac® 2 Lamp. Based on an original lamp in the Dana-Thomas House, sixteen panels fan out to recall prairie sumac.

TALIESIN WOOD LAMP (H)

Cherry, with wine or walnut finish. Floor, table, and hanging variations. Yamagiwa. Taliesin® 2, 3, and Pendant Lamps. These glassless boxes positioned around a spine project soft, indirect light.

PAGODA-SHADE LAMP (I)

Cherry or ash with various finishes. Table and floor variations. Yamagiwa. Taliesin® 1 Table and Floor Lamps. Many of these square lamps, with their Japanese-style shades, can still be found at Taliesin.

STORER FLOOR LAMP (J)

Painted steel and frosted glass. 6' 4" high, 6 ¹⁄₁₆" wide, 8" deep. Yamagiwa. Storer® 1 Floor Lamp. The square light and a matching sconce mimic the concrete blocks used in the Storer House (1923).

GUGGENHEIM TEAPOT AND COFFEE SET (A)

Porcelain. Teapot, mugs, and espresso and cappuccino cups and saucers. Krups. These table items take their spiraling shape from Wright's Solomon R. Guggenheim Museum (1943–59) in New York.

DAVID WRIGHT DESERT SET (B)

Porcelain. Dessert plates and mugs. Swid Powell for the Museum of Modern Art. A 1951 rug that Wright designed for his son's Arizona home inspired the swirling circular motifs on this colorful set.

TREE OF LIFE PANEL (C)

Iridescent glass. 12 7/8" high, 8 1/2" wide. Classmasters. This geometric rendition of three trees in bloom appears in banks of windows under the roofline and elsewhere at Wright's Darwin Martin House.

DANA BUTTERFLY DETAIL (D)

Iridescent glass. 5 1/2" high, 19 1/8" wide. Classmasters. Semicircular transoms filled with colorful art glass butterflies greet visitors to the Dana-Thomas House. A portion is now available for display at home.

OAK PARK SKYLIGHT PANEL (E)

Iridescent glass. 13 3/8" high, 6 3/8" wide. Classmasters. Wright created the effect of an autumn forest in his studio with this green-and-gold skylight, which can be hung or displayed on a tabletop.

SAGUARO GLASS PANEL (F)

Iridescent glass. 11 7/8" high, 11" wide. Classmasters. Inspired by flowering desert cactus, Wright designed a cover for *Liberty* magazine in 1926 that was executed in glass at the Arizona Biltmore in 1973.

COONLEY PLAYHOUSE CLERESTORY (G)

Clear and flashed opal glass with zinc channels. 17 7/8" high, 33 3/4" wide. Oakbrook Esser Studios. Clerestory I. Installed as a window or displayed, this recalls the balloons, flags, and confetti of a parade.

ROBIE HOUSE WINDOW (H)

Iridescent glass with copper channels. 43 7/8" high, 31 1/8" wide. Oakbrook Esser Studios. Robie® I. This Prairie-style favorite can be paired with three other window patterns from the Robie House.

ART GLASS WINDOWS (I)

Antique glass with zinc channels. Various sizes. Andersen Windows. Four designs are available as windows: Colonnade (shown, from Wright's Unity Temple), Prairie Rhythm, Wichita, and Eucalyptus.

MIDWAY GARDENS DANCING GLASS (J)

Clear and opal glass with zinc channels. 32 1/2" high, 33 1/2" wide. Oakbrook Esser Studios. Triangles enliven this window that Wright designed for Midway Gardens, one of several features never made.

C

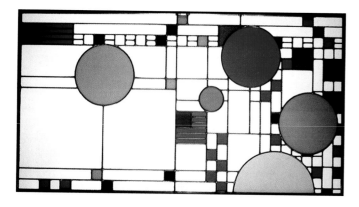

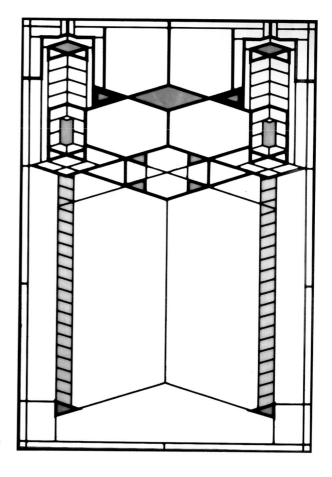

H

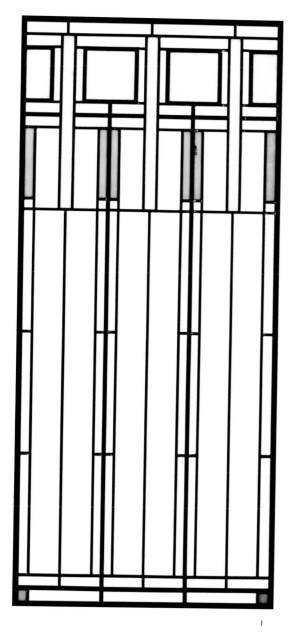

I

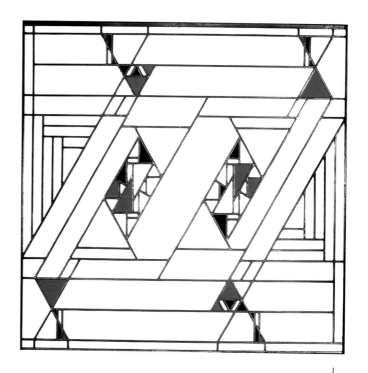

J

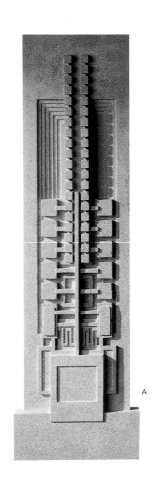

A

B

C

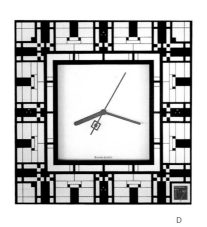

D

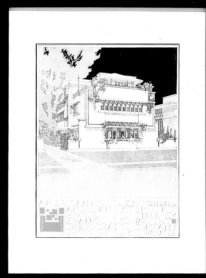

E

F

C

H

I

J

HOLLYHOCK PANEL (A)

Concrete. 28" high, 7 ¾" wide. Omnia. Abstract hollyhocks in art stone form a roofline frieze on Wright's Hollyhock House. A single panel of this distinctive motif has been reproduced ready to hang.

FROEBEL GIFTS (B)

Maple. Uncle Goose. A reproduction of the learning materials that set Wright on his architectural path as a boy, this set includes 95 natural maple blocks and a design grid on which to place them.

METAL PICTURE FRAMES (C)

Various finishes. 3" square and 4" x 6" openings. Museum of Modern Art. Various motifs from Wright buildings, including Taliesin and the Robie, Coonley, and Storer Houses, are available as frames.

STUDIO WINDOW WALL CLOCK (D)

Mirrored glass. 12" square, 1½" deep. Bulova. An adaptation of the art glass window in Wright's office in his Oak Park studio, this wall clock includes the architect's red signature block at the bottom.

FRAMED HOUSE PRINT (E)

Wood framed. 19" high, 15" wide. Museum of Modern Art. An exterior elevation shows one of Wright's earliest ideas for standardized construction: the American System-Built Houses of 1915-17.

VELVET PILLOWS (F)

Rayon silk velvet in spruce, gold, and scarlet. 16" square. Rivertown Trading Company. Patterns from Wright's Moore House and the Lake Geneva Inn (1911) reflect motifs used in his Prairie buildings.

TULIP MAGAZINE RACK (G)

Aluminum with matte finish. 13½" high, 11" wide, 9" deep. Rivertown Trading Company. This diamond-based tulip design is taken from Wright's Lake Geneva Inn, a Wisconsin resort since demolished.

CLEMATIS VINE RUG (H)

Wool. Custom sizes and colors. Patterson, Flynn and Martin/Schumacher. Featuring summer foliage, this two-tone vine pattern was inspired by Wright's love of nature and Japanese art and culture.

MARTIN SENOUR PAINT COLORS (I)

Six palettes. Martin Senour. Continuing the line announced in *House Beautiful* in 1955 are 36 hues in palettes such as Adobe Earth, Reeds and Grasses, Mountain Scape, Sierra Sunset, and Sand Dune Dusk.

SCHUMACHER WALLPAPERS AND FABRICS (J)

Various materials. Schumacher. First launched in *House Beautiful's* November 1955 issue, this latest line featuring 30 patterns abstracts popular Wright motifs such as grasses, vines, ferns, sumac, wisteria, maple leaves, pine bark, and waterfalls.

COPPER URN (A)

Copper. 9" and 18" high. Historical Arts and Casting. Interlocking circular and square motifs distinguish this famous vase that Wright made about 1898. He used it for many clients as well as for himself.

COPPER WEED HOLDER (B)

Copper. 29" high. Historical Arts and Casting. Because he liked to display dried natural flowers at home, Wright devised this sinuous four-sided vase about 1895. Photographs show it in his own studio.

MINIC SQUARE VASE (C)

Cast bronze. 8" square. Historical Arts and Casting. Designed to be made of olive wood with a copper liner, this vase was shown in the November 1955 *House Beautiful* for use with Wright's furniture line.

MINIC DUO VASE (D)

Cast bronze. 21" high, 7 ½" wide. Historical Arts and Casting. A prototype of this double vase was also published in the November 1955 *House Beautiful,* but it has only recently been manufactured.

DANA SUMAC VASE (E)

Glazed terra cotta. 11 ¾" high, 5 ¾" base (half original size). D&D Volker Enterprises. Dana House Sumac® Vase. A tall Teco vase with Wright's sumac design sat on Susan Lawrence Dana's hearth.

FURNISHING SOURCES

General information: Archetype Associates (212-777-9080)

Mail-Order Catalogues

Frank Lloyd Wright Home and Studio Foundation
951 Chicago Avenue
Oak Park, Ill. 60302-2097
877-848-3559; fax 708-848-2327
www.wrightcatalogue.org

Rivertown Trading Company
1000 Westgate Drive
St. Paul, Minn. 55114-1077
800-735-2587; fax 651-645-7092

Major Retail Outlets

Art Institute of Chicago
111 South Michigan Avenue
Chicago, Ill. 60603
800-621-9337; fax 847-299-8286

Dana-Thomas House Sumac Shop
301 East Lawrence Avenue
Springfield, Ill. 62703
217-744-3598; fax 217-788-9450

Museum of Modern Art
11 West 53rd Street
New York, N.Y. 10019-5401
800-447-6662; fax 610-431-3333
www.moma.org

Taliesin Visitor Center
P. O. Box 399
Spring Green, Wis. 53588
608-588-7900; fax 608-588-7514

Taliesin West
12621 North Frank Lloyd Wright Boulevard
Scottsdale, Ariz. 85259
480-860-2700, extension 221; fax 480-860-8472

Manufacturers

Andersen Windows
P.O. Box 203070
Austin, Tex. 78720-9751
800-426-4261, extension 1232

Bulova
One Bulova Drive
Woodside, N.Y. 11377-7874
800-228-5682; fax 718-204-3414

Cassina USA
200 McKay Road
Huntington Station, N.Y. 11746
516-423-4560; fax 516-423-5245

Classmasters/Omnia
2501 Mechanicsville Turnpike
Richmond, Va. 23223
800-488-2494; fax 804-648-7839

Historical Arts and Casting
5580 West Bagley Park Road
West Jordan, Utah 84088
800-225-1414; fax 801-280-2493
www.historicalarts.com

Krups
7 Reuten Drive
Closter, N.J. 07624
800-526-5377; fax 201-767-5634

Nichols Bros. Stoneworks
20209 Broadway
Snohomish, Wash. 98290
800-483-5720; fax 425-483-5721

Martin Senour Company
101 Prospect Avenue, N.W.
Cleveland, Ohio 41115
800-677-5270; fax 216-566-1655

Oakbrook Esser Studios
129 East Wisconsin Avenue
Oconomowoc, Wis. 53066
800-223-5193; fax 262-567-6487

F. Schumacher and Company
79 Madison Avenue
New York, N.Y. 10016
800-523-1200 (information)
212-415-3900 (showroom)
fax 212-213-7848
www.fschumacher.com

D&D Volker Enterprises
P.O. Box 649
Sadler, Tex. 76264
800-443-4683; fax 415-472-6473

Yamagiwa USA
31310 Via Colinas, Unit 106
Westlake Village, Calif. 91362
888-879-8611; fax 818-879-8640

SOURCES AND ACKNOWLEDGMENTS

The two most important sources used in the preparation of *Frank Lloyd Wright's House Beautiful* were Wright's own statements of his principles in speeches and writings and issues of *House Beautiful* presenting Wright's work.

Wright first set out to codify his architectural philosophy in "The Architect and the Machine," a speech given in 1894 to the University Guild in suburban Evanston, Illinois. Two years later, in 1896, he returned there to restate his themes in a talk entitled "Architect, Architecture, and the Client," in which he walked listeners through his vision of a perfect house. An essay "In the Cause of Architecture" in the March 1908 *Architectural Record* revisited his 1894 ideas in particular and began a series of essays under this title published over the years, most notably in 1927 and 1928. Wright joined drawings and words in three features published in the *Ladies' Home Journal* in 1901 and 1907: "A Home in a Prairie Town," "A Small House with 'Lots of Room in It,'" and "A Fireproof House for $5,000." In a 1910 monograph presenting more of his drawings, *Ausgeführte Bauten und Entwürfe von Frank Lloyd Wright* (known as the Wasmuth edition of his drawings and plans), the architect made a profound impact in Europe as he explained the tenets of his new architecture for democracy. His respect for Japanese prints and their underlying culture was described in *The Japanese Print: An Interpretation,* a book published in 1912 by Ralph Fletcher Seymour.

In May 1930 Wright related his views on everything from houses to skyscrapers in six lectures to Princeton undergraduates, published in 1931 as *Modern Architecture, Being the Kahn Lectures* (Princeton University). Wright's most personal statement was *An Autobiography* (Longmans, Green), published in 1932 as a means to redirect his life and career. Part architectural treatise, part romance, it brought Wright new clients fascinated by his ideas and swashbuckling style. A revised edition in 1943 (Duell, Sloan and Pearce) expanded the story of his life and work.

In his last years Wright summed up his lifelong principles in several important books. *The Natural House* (Horizon Press) of 1954 is a clear restatement of views on residential design first uttered in 1894, strengthened by descriptions of how he was building modern houses for Usonia. In 1957 Wright, then ninety, produced a testimonial to his life's work in *A Testament* (Horizon Press). A year before his death, *The Living City* (Horizon Press) of 1958 made one last plea for an architecture in harmony with nature.

Wright's speeches and publications have been compiled into five volumes entitled *Frank Lloyd Wright: Collected Writings* (New York: Rizzoli, 1992–95), edited by Bruce Brooks Pfeiffer. Excerpts from Wright's writings are also now available in a new edition of *An American Architecture: Frank Lloyd Wright* (Barnes and Noble Books, 1998), edited by Edgar Kaufmann Jr. and first published in 1955 by Horizon Press. For making these and other words of Wright so readily available, Pfeiffer, who is the director of the Frank Lloyd Wright Archives, deserves the gratitude of everyone who researches and admires Wright's work. References in this book's text to Wright's views by date come from the sources indicated above.

Numerous issues of *House Beautiful* over six decades provide contemporaneous insights into Wright's impact at different points of his career. The magazine identified a new architectural genius during visits to Wright's home and studio in its issues of February 1897 ("Successful Houses. III") and December 1899 ("An Architect's Studio"). In 1906 it revisited Wright in June ("A House on a Bluff"), July ("Making the Most of a Narrow Lot"), and August ("A House without a Servant") to survey progressive ideas in three of his Prairie houses. An August 1911 article on "Housing the Automobile" pictured Wright's stable-garage for his publishing partner, William Winslow. In June 1946, to see what he had been up to in the intervening years, the magazine invited readers to "Meet Frank Lloyd Wright," and then in December 1946, to celebrate *House Beautiful's* fiftieth anniversary, the editors went to Taliesin West to visit "The Most Influential Design Source of the Last 50 Years." Loren Pope disclosed "The Love Affair of a Man and His House" in August 1948. Editor Elizabeth Gordon rallied supporters of natural houses with her anti-International Style editorial in the April 1953 issue ("The Threat to the Next America"). The magazine gave Wright a forum to expound on the same subject in July ("Frank Lloyd Wright Speaks Up") and October 1953 ("For a Democratic Architecture"). A year later, in October 1954, *House Beautiful* explained that it had dedicated *The Arts of Daily Living,* an exhibition at the Los Angeles County Fair, to Wright. An ambitious special issue ("His Contribution to the Beauty of American Life") in November 1955 brought Wright's principles to a new generation of homeowners and was bound in a special hardcover edition. "A New Era of Romanticism" in home design, based on Wright's work, was heralded in May 1956. Two of his innovative commissions in the Southwest were profiled in November 1956 ("The Look of American Life at the Top Level"). The magazine called Wright "Our Strongest Influence for Enrichment" in January 1957, and in October 1959 another special issue ("Your Heritage from Frank Lloyd Wright") paid tribute to him five months after his death. Describing the Hanna House in a January 1963 special issue, *House Beautiful* showed "How a Great Frank Lloyd Wright House Changed, Grew, Came to Perfection."

On the 125th anniversary of Wright's birth, Jane Margolies of the magazine staff joined four of the architect's colleagues in June 1992 in "Remembering Mr. Wright"; other features were also devoted to his work. For the magazine's own centennial in November 1996, Christine Pittel and Martin Filler recounted in

House Beautiful a century of design in which Wright's work played such an important role. In "Meeting Mr. Wright," Jane Margolies encouraged Elizabeth Gordon to reminisce about her eventful years with Wright.

Back issues of the magazine were reviewed at the Frank Lloyd Wright Archives, Library of Congress, New York Public Library, and offices of *House Beautiful.* Much appreciation is due Penny Fowler of the Frank Lloyd Wright Foundation, Deborah Martin of *House Beautiful,* Alison Maddex, and Robert Vogel for their assistance with this research. Penny Fowler, along with Kate Henselmans and Steve Kroeter of Archetype Associates, also assisted with compilation of the book's furnishings catalogue.

The correspondence between Wright and Elizabeth Gordon of *House Beautiful* in the 1940s and 1950s offers illuminating insights into their close but sometimes prickly relationship (as was typical for Wright). I am grateful to the Frank Lloyd Wright Archives for providing access to this resource and to Sara Hammond for aid in locating key documents. Indira Berndtson was generous in sharing Jane Margolies's 1992 interview with John deKoven Hill regarding his tenure at *House Beautiful* as well as her own 1996 interview with René Carrillo about his work on Schumacher's Taliesin Line in 1955. Bruce Brooks Pfeiffer, Oskar Muñoz, Suzette Lucas, and Margo Stipe of the Foundation provided useful information and assistance.

Virginia T. Boyd has written previously about Wright and *House Beautiful* in "The House Beautiful: Frank Lloyd Wright for Everyone," in the Elvehjem Museum of Art *Bulletin* (Madison, Wis.: Elvehjem Museum of Art, 1987–88) and in "House Beautiful and Frank Lloyd Wright," in *The Frank Lloyd Wright Quarterly* (Scottsdale, Ariz.: Frank Lloyd Wright Foundation, Fall 1997), publications shared by the Frank Lloyd Wright Archives during research for this book.

Views relevant to Wright's own design principles can be found in William C. Gannett's *The House Beautiful,* which Wright designed in 1896 and which has been reissued (Rohnert Park, Calif.: Pomegranate, 1996) with a new foreword by John Arthur. For a more detailed understanding of period visions of the house beautiful, the work of Gwendolyn Wright is highly recommended, notably *Moralism and the Model Home: Domestic Architecture and Cultural Conflict in Chicago, 1873–1913* (Chicago: University of Chicago Press, 1980); "Frank Lloyd Wright and the Domestic Landscape," in *Frank Lloyd Wright: Architect* (New York: Museum of Modern Art, 1994); and "Architectural Practice and Social Vision in Wright's Early Designs," in *The Nature of Frank Lloyd Wright,* edited by Carol R. Bolen (Chicago: University of Chicago Press, 1988). Another good source on the era is Delores Hayden's *Redesigning the American Dream: The Future of Housing, Work, and Family Life* (New York: W. W. Norton, 1984).

Many other scholars have paved the way for study of Wright's work and amassed a large body of informative publications. For those who want to know how and why Wright's buildings work, *Frank Lloyd Wright: A Primer on Architectural Principles*, edited by Robert McCarter (New York: Princeton Architectural Press, 1991) is a rich lode of theories. Donald Hoffmann's *Understanding Frank Lloyd Wright's Architecture* (New York: Dover Publications, 1995) is a thoughtful analysis more accessible to general readers, as are all of Hoffmann's books on Wright.

Several recent comprehensive books tackle a wide range of issues on Wright. Among those consulted were *Frank Lloyd Wright: Architect*, edited by Terence Riley with Peter Reed (New York: Museum of Modern Art, 1994); *The Architecture of Frank Lloyd Wright*, by Neil Levine (Princeton: Princeton University Press, 1996); and *Frank Lloyd Wright*, by Robert McCarter (London: Phaidon Press, 1997).

John Sergeant's *Frank Lloyd Wright's Usonian Houses: The Case for Organic Architecture* (New York: Whitney Library of Design, 1976) laid the groundwork for study of these moderate-cost houses. An illustrated synopsis of Wright's Usonian principles appeared in the September 1956 issue of *House and Home. The Pope-Leighey House* (Washington, D.C.: National Trust for Historic Preservation, 1969), edited by Terry B. Morton, who first introduced me to Wright, offers a case study of one house featured in *House Beautiful.*

For a concise catalogue of all of Wright's built projects, including plans, William Allin Storrer's *Frank Lloyd Wright Companion* (Chicago: University of Chicago Press, 1993) is the standard reference. Meryle Secrest's biography *Frank Lloyd Wright* (New York: Knopf, 1992) presents the long and complex story of Wright's ninety-one years of life.

The books written by Carla Lind for Archetype Press—*The Wright Style* (New York: Simon and Schuster, 1992), the Wright at a Glance Series (Rohnert Park, Calif.: Pomegranate, 1994–96), and *Lost Wright: Frank Lloyd Wright's Vanished Masterpieces* (New York: Simon and Schuster, 1996)—have provided continual sources of inspiration over the years. For her model of how to bring Wright to life, I am most grateful of all. My other Wright authors, Pedro E. Guerrero (Wright's photographer) and Dixie Legler, also perpetually keep me in the Wright frame of mind. And Loren Pope shows that "The Love Affair of a Man and His House," which he described in *House Beautiful* in 1948, need never end.

Elizabeth Rice, editorial director of Hearst Books, has shared my enthusiasm for Wright's ideal of the house beautiful. Robert Wiser, my designer, has once again captured the Wright style with precision. And my other Robert is always just right.

Diane Maddex

FURTHER READING

In addition to the sources outlined on pages 172–73, the following books about Frank Lloyd Wright are recommended:

Alofsin, Anthony. *Frank Lloyd Wright: The Lost Years, 1910–1922.* Chicago: University of Chicago Press, 1993.

Brooks, H. Allen. *The Prairie School: Frank Lloyd Wright and His Midwest Contemporaries.* 1972. Reprint, New York: W. W. Norton, 1976.

Guerrero, Pedro E. *Picturing Wright: An Album from Frank Lloyd Wright's Photographer.* Rohnert Park, Calif.: Pomegranate, 1994.

Hanks, David A. *The Decorative Designs of Frank Lloyd Wright.* 1979. Reprint, New York: Dover Publications, 1999.

Hanna, Paul and Jean. *Frank Lloyd Wright's Hanna House: The Client's Report.* Cambridge: MIT Press, 1981.

Hitchcock, Henry-Russell. *In the Nature of Materials: The Buildings of Frank Lloyd Wright, 1887–1941.* 1942. Reprint, New York: Da Capo, 1969.

Hoffmann, Donald. *Frank Lloyd Wright: Architecture and Nature,* New York: Dover Publications, 1986.

Kaufmann, Edgar, Jr. *Fallingwater: A Frank Lloyd Wright Country House.* New York: Abbeville, 1986.

Legler, Dixie. *Prairie Style: Houses and Gardens by Frank Lloyd Wright and the Prairie School.* New York: Stewart, Tabori and Chang, 1999.

Maddex, Diane. *50 Favorite Furnishings by Frank Lloyd Wright.* New York: Smithmark Publishers, 1999.

———. *50 Favorite Houses by Frank Lloyd Wright.* New York: Smithmark Publishers, 2000.

———. *50 Favorite Rooms by Frank Lloyd Wright.* New York: Smithmark Publishers, 1998.

Manson, Grant Carpenter. *Frank Lloyd Wright to 1910: The First Golden Age.* New York: Van Nostrand Reinhold, 1958.

Nute, Kevin. *Frank Lloyd Wright and Japan.* New York: Van Nostrand Reinhold, 1993.

Pfeiffer, Bruce Brooks. *Frank Lloyd Wright.* 1991. Reprint, New York: Barnes and Noble Books, 1994.

———. *Frank Lloyd Wright: The Masterworks.* New York: Rizzoli, 1993.

Pfeiffer, Bruce Brooks, ed. *Frank Lloyd Wright Complete Works.* Tokyo: ADA Edita, 1987–88.

———. *Frank Lloyd Wright Selected Houses.* Tokyo: ADA Edita, 1991–93.

Sweeney, Robert L. *Wright in Hollywood: Visions of a New Architecture.* Architectural History Foundation. Cambridge: MIT Press, 1994.

INDEX